CW0571122

WOK COOKBOOK

365 days of Delicious, Easy and Traditional Wok Recipes with Modern Twists for Home Cooks | For Beginners and Advanced Users

WANG JEN

TABLE OF CONTENTS

INTRODUCTION

In "The Wok Cookbook," you'll find recipes throughout Asia. For millennia, Asians have relied on the wok, a multipurpose and iconic cooking pan, to prepare delicious and nutritious food at the centre of many regional cuisines.

This cookbook features various dishes highlighting the many tastes, textures, and preparation methods found in Asian cooking. This cookbook provides something delicious for everyone, whether looking for a hearty bowl of soup or a plate of crunchy fried noodles.

This book is written for experienced cooks and those just starting who want to learn how to use a wok to create authentic Chinese and other Asian dishes at home. Aside from picking out, seasoning, and caring for your wok, you'll also pick up on the wok's cultural importance and historical background along the way.

With the help of this cookbook, you can prepare healthful and flavorful dishes with an Asian twist that will wow your loved ones. Get out your wok and kitchen shears because we're about to start cooking.

CHAPTER 1
INTRODUCTION TO WOK COOKING

L et's talk about wok cooking, a technique that has been integral to Asian food for decades. The wok, a one-of-a-kind cooking pan, is widely used throughout Asia to prepare a broad range of tasty and nutritious foods.

History and Culture of Wok Cooking

The wok was first used in China for cooking over open flames, but its history goes far further. The wok has become an indispensable kitchen utensil in many parts of Asia, including China, Japan, Korea, Thailand, and Vietnam.

The use of a wok is ingrained in the history and culture of many Asian countries. It's often connected with parties, holidays, and other joyous events. The wok symbolizes wealth, good fortune, and hospitality in many Asian cultures.

Different Types of Woks

Several distinct varieties of woks are commercially available, each with its own set of certain advantages and drawbacks. Some of the most typical woks are:

Carbon Steel Wok

One of the most common types of woks used by chefs is made of carbon steel. It's strong, easy to carry, and becomes hot very rapidly.

Cast Iron Wok

Cast-iron woks are perfect for high-temperature cooking because they are hefty and hold heat efficiently.

Stainless Steel Wok

Third, a stainless steel wok is a contemporary option since it is durable and simple to care for. Those with a nickel allergy will also find it a suitable alternative.

Non-Stick Wok

Non-stick woks are covered with a non-stick substance, making them simple to clean after use. However, it should not be subjected to very hot cooking conditions.

Selecting the Best Wok

Take into account your cooking habits and preferences when deciding on a wok. Consider your family size, the capacity of your stove, and the foods you want to prepare.

If you want your wok to last long and stay in excellent shape, you should season it and take good care of it.

The use of the wok is an integral part of the culinary heritage of many Asian countries. The correct wok and some fundamental cooking skills can allow you to wow your loved ones with nutritious and flavorful dishes. What are you waiting for? Give wok cooking a go right now and see what all the fuss is about.

CHAPTER 2
BASIC WOK TECHNIQUES

Wok cooking is renowned for its speed and efficiency, yielding delicious and nutritious meals. Some of the most important aspects of wok cooking, such as stir-frying, deep-frying, steaming, and smoking, will be discussed in this chapter.

Stir-Frying

Quick and straightforward, stir-frying entails frying food in tiny batches in a wok over high heat with a small quantity of oil. To guarantee consistent cooking and avoid sticking, frequent swirling and tossing are required while using this method.

The wok has to be sizzling hot before you can begin your stir-fry. Put some oil in the wok and stir it around to cover the inside. Stir-fry the ingredients for a few minutes in the wok until they are done.

Deep-Frying

In order to get a crunchy texture in foods like tempura, fried chicken, and spring rolls, deep-frying is a common cooking method. Deep-frying requires a lot of oil, which must be heated to a high temperature in a wok. Throw everything in the pan and fry it until it's nice, brown, and crispy.

When deep-frying, use caution to avoid oil splatters and burning. Remove the food from the wok using a slotted spoon or spider and set it on a paper towel to absorb any remaining oil.

Steaming

Fish, vegetables, and dumplings are some of the most typical foods cooked by steaming since they are nutritious and low-fat. Boil the water to create steam. Add the food to be cooked to a bamboo steamer or steaming rack set in a wok. Put a lid on the wok and steam the meal for a few minutes until it's done.

Smoking

Food may be smoked to give it a Smokey taste by being exposed to the smoke of burning wood chips, tea leaves, or herbs. A wok may be used for smoking if aluminum foil is used to line the bottom and the smoking material is placed on top. To smoke food, heat the wok with the smoking material until it starts to smoke, then add the meal. Leave the wok covered for a few minutes to allow the food to absorb the smoke.

The secret to making delicious wok food is to master these fundamental methods. Your taste buds and body will thanks for your time and effort you put into mastering the techniques of stir-frying, deep-frying, steaming, and smoking. Now, bring out your wok and help me make dinner!

CHAPTER 3
RICE AND NOODLES

1. Yangzhou Fried Rice

Items used:

- 3 cups cooked jasmine rice, a day old
- 3 eggs, lightly beaten
- 1/2 cup diced ham
- 1/2 cup cooked shrimp, peeled and deveined
- 1/2 cup frozen peas
- 2 scallions, thinly sliced
- 2 tablespoons vegetable oil
- 1 tablespoon soy sauce
- Salt and pepper to taste

How to cook:

Prepare a high heat in a big skillet or wok. Coat the pan with the vegetable oil and add it.

Second, pour in the beaten eggs and scramble until they are done. Take out of the frying pan.

Third, stir-fry the diced ham for a minute or two, or until it begins to brown.

Then, after 2 minutes of stir-frying, toss in the shrimp that have been cooked and frozen peas.

Cooked jasmine rice should be added to a pan and stir-fried for two to three minutes to reheat.

Scramble the eggs, return them to the pan, and mix everything.

To taste, add soy sauce, mineral salt, and pepper.

Serve immediately while still hot, and top with chopped scallions.

Nutrients:

Calories: 360

Fat: 14g

Carbohydrates: 40g

Protein: 17g

2. Chicken Chow Mein

Items used:

- 12 oz thin egg noodles
- 1 lb boneless, skinless chicken breast, sliced into thin strips
- 2 cups bok choy, chopped
- 1 cup mushrooms, sliced
- 1 cup bean sprouts
- 2 cloves garlic, minced
- 2 tablespoons vegetable oil
- Salt and pepper to taste

For the sauce:

- 1/4 cup soy sauce
- 2 tablespoons oyster sauce
- 1 tablespoon hoisin sauce

- 1 tablespoon cornstarch
- 1 tablespoon water

How to cook:

First, prepare the egg noodles as directed on the box. Drain and put away.

Soy sauce, oyster sauce, hoisin sauce, corn starch, and water are combined in a small basin and whisked together to form the sauce.

Third, heat the vegetable oil to very high temperatures in a big skillet or wok. Stir-fry the chicken for three to four minutes until it is browned and fully done.

After around 2 minutes of stir-frying the cloves of garlic, bok choy, mushrooms, and bean sprouts may be added to the pan.

Stir in the prepared egg noodles to mix everything in the pan.

Once your delicious sauce has reduced and thickened, pour it over the noodles and continue to stir-fry for another minute or two, at which point the noodles and veggies will be well-coated.

Add a little pepper and salt to taste.

Keep the food hot.

Nutrients:

Calories: 450

Fat: 12g

Carbohydrates: 50g

Protein: 35g

3. Pad Thai

Items used:

- 8 oz rice noodles
- 1/2 lb shrimp, peeled and deveined
- 1/2 cup firm tofu, diced
- 1 cup bean sprouts

- 2 eggs, lightly beaten
- 2 cloves garlic, minced
- 2 tablespoons vegetable oil
- 1/4 cup roasted peanuts, chopped
- 2 tablespoons chopped scallions
- Lime wedges, for serving

For the sauce:

- 3 tablespoons tamarind paste
- 2 tablespoons fish sauce
- 2 tablespoons brown sugar
- 1 tablespoon soy sauce
- 1/4 teaspoon red pepper flakes

How to cook:

Rice noodles must be soaked in boiling water for up to 15 minutes until they soften. Drain and put away.

Tamarind paste, fish sauce, brown sugar, vinegar, soy sauce, and red pepper flakes are whisked together in a small basin.

Vegetable oil should be heated in a wok or big pan over high heat. Put in the garlic and cook for a minute or two until it smells good.

Stir-fry the shrimp and tofu for 2–3 minutes, or until the shrimp become pink and are fully cooked.

The eggs should be added to the empty side of the pan, while the shrimp and tofu are pushed to one side. The eggs need to be scrambled until they're done.

Cooked rice noodles should be added to the pan and mixed.

Stir-fry the noodles and veggies for a further minute after pouring on the sauce, until the sauce thickens and covers everything.

Stir in the chopped peanuts and bean sprouts to mix.

Put in as much salt and pepper as you want.

Serve hot with lime wedges and garnish with chopped scallions.

Nutrients:

Calories: 450

Fat: 18g

Carbohydrates: 50g

Protein: 20g

4. Beef Fried Rice

Items used:

- 3 cups cooked white rice, preferably leftover and chilled
- 1/2 lb thinly sliced beef
- 1 cup frozen peas and carrots
- 1/2 cup corn kernels
- 2 cloves garlic, minced
- 2 tablespoons vegetable oil
- 2 tablespoons soy sauce
- 1 tablespoon oyster sauce
- Salt and pepper to taste

How to cook:

Vegetable oil should be heated in a wok or big pan over high heat. Stir-fry the garlic mince for a minute or two, or until fragrant.

Stir-fry the beef slices for 2 to 3 minutes or until it is browned and cooked all the way through.

Stir-fry the meat for another minute before adding the frozen peas, carrots, and corn kernels.

Cooked white rice should be added to the pan and mixed.

After the rice has been stir-fried for 1-2 minutes, sprinkle the soy sauce and oyster sauce over the top.

Put in as much salt and pepper as you want.

A hot dish is what you need.

Nutrients:

Calories: 400

Fat: 12g

Carbohydrates: 50g

Protein: 20g

5. Dan Dan Noodles

Items used:

- 8 oz Chinese wheat noodles
- 1/2 lb ground pork
- 2 tablespoons vegetable oil
- 2 cloves garlic, minced
- 2 tablespoons chili oil
- 1 tablespoon Sichuan peppercorns, toasted and ground
- 2 tablespoons soy sauce
- 2 tablespoons black vinegar
- 2 tablespoons sugar
- 1/2 cup scallions, thinly sliced

How to cook:

Prepare the Chinese noodles made from wheat as directed on the box. Drain and put away.

Vegetable oil should be heated in a wok or big pan over high heat. Stir-fry the garlic mince for a minute or two, or until fragrant.

The ground pork should be added to the pan and stir-fried for about 3 to 4 minutes, or until it is finely browned and heated.

Stir-fry again for two to three minutes, then add the Chile oil and Sichuan peppercorns.

Cooked Chinese noodles made of wheat should be added to the pan.

Stir-fry the noodles for a further minute after adding the soy sauce, black vinegar, and sugar, until the noodles are cooked through and covered in the sauce.

Put in as much salt and pepper as you want.

Serve immediately with chopped scallions as a garnish.

Nutrients:

Calories: 450

Fat: 20g

Carbohydrates: 45g

Protein: 20g

6. Vegetable Lo Mein

Items used:

- 8 oz egg noodles
- 1 cup broccoli florets
- 1 cup sliced carrots
- 1 cup sliced bell peppers
- 1/2 cup sliced mushrooms
- 2 cloves garlic, minced
- 2 tablespoons vegetable oil
- 2 tablespoons soy sauce
- 1 tablespoon oyster sauce
- Salt and pepper to taste

How to cook:

Egg noodles should be prepared by package directions. Drain and put away.

Vegetable oil should be heated in a wok or big pan over high heat. Stir-fry the garlic mince for a minute or two, or until fragrant.

Stir-fry the florets of broccoli, carrots, bell peppers, and mushrooms for 2–3 minutes, or until the veggies are soft.

Stir add the cooked egg noodles to the skillet.

Stir-fry the noodles and veggies for a further minute or two after you add the soy sauce and oyster sauce to ensure the noodles are cooked through and covered with the sauce.

Put in as much salt and pepper as you want.

A hot dish is what you need.

Nutrients:

Calories: 350

Fat: 10g

Carbohydrates: 55g

Protein: 10g

7. Chicken Pad See Ew

Items used:

- 16 oz wide rice noodles
- 1 lb boneless chicken thighs, sliced into thin strips
- 4 cups broccoli florets
- 4 garlic cloves, minced
- 2 tbsp vegetable oil
- 2 tbsp soy sauce
- 2 tbsp oyster sauce
- 2 tbsp brown sugar
- 1/4 tsp white pepper

How to cook:

Rice noodles must be softened by soaking in hot water for 30 minutes. Drain and put away.

Soy sauce, oyster sauce, brown sugar, and white pepper should be combined in a small basin.

Putting aside.

Place the wok over high flame and add the vegetable oil. Put in the garlic and cook for a minute or two until it smells good.

Slice up some chicken breasts, then stir-fry them for three to four minutes, or until they are no longer pink in the middle.

To make tender-crisp broccoli, add it to the frying pan and stir-fry for 3 to 4 minutes.

Stir-fry the rice noodles and sauce for two to three minutes, or until the noodles are tender and the sauce is absorbed.

If preferred, serve the Chicken Pad See Ew hot, with chopped onions or cilantro.

Nutritional Information:

Calories: 475

Fat: 13g

Carbohydrates: 67g

Protein: 26g

8. Kimchi Fried Rice

Items used:

- 2 cups cooked and chilled white rice
- 1/2 cup kimchi, chopped
- 2 eggs, lightly beaten
- 2 cloves garlic, minced
- 2 tablespoons vegetable oil
- 1 tablespoon soy sauce
- 1 tablespoon sesame oil
- 1/2 cup scallions, thinly sliced

How to cook:

Vegetable oil should be heated in a wok or big pan over high heat. Stir-fry the garlic mince for a minute or two, or until fragrant.

Stir-fry the chopped kimchi for 2–3 minutes, or until it is hot throughout.

Cooked white rice should be added to the pan and mixed.

After the rice has been stir-fried for 1-2 minutes, pour the soy sauce and sesame oil over it to ensure it is evenly coated and heated.

You can add the eggs to the other side of the pan by pushing the rice to one side. The eggs need to be scrambled until they're done.

Scramble the eggs and add them to the rice.

Put in as much salt and pepper as you want.

Serve immediately with chopped scallions as a garnish.

Nutrients:

Calories: 400

Fat: 18g

Carbohydrates: 45g

Protein: 12g

9. Singapore Noodles

Items used:

- 8 oz thin rice noodles
- 1/2 lb shrimp, peeled and deveined
- 1 red bell pepper, thinly sliced
- 1 yellow onion, thinly sliced
- 2 cloves garlic, minced
- 2 tablespoons vegetable oil
- 1 tablespoon curry powder
- 2 tablespoons soy sauce
- 2 tablespoons rice vinegar

- Salt and pepper to taste

How to cook:

Thin rice noodles should be prepared by the package's directions. Drain and put away.

Vegetable oil should be heated in a wok or big pan over high heat. Stir-fry the garlic mince for a minute or two, or until fragrant.

To make the red bell pepper and yellow onion soft, add them to the pan and stir-fry for 2 to 3 minutes.

Stir-fry for another 2–3 minutes, or until the shrimp are pink and opaque throughout, after adding the shrimp that has been peeled and deveined.

Cooked thin rice noodles should be added to the pan and mixed.

Stir-fry the noodles and veggies for a further minute or two after you add the curry powder, soy sauce, and rice vinegar. This will ensure the noodles are well cooked and covered with the sauce.

Put in as much salt and pepper as you want.

A hot dish is what you need.

Nutrients:

Calories: 400

Fat: 12g

Carbohydrates: 50g

Protein: 20g

10. Shrimp Fried Rice

Items used:

- 3 cups cooked white rice, preferably leftover and chilled
- 1/2 lb shrimp, peeled and deveined
- 1 cup frozen peas and carrots, defrosted
- 1/2 cup diced onion

- 2 cloves garlic, minced
- 2 tablespoons vegetable oil
- 2 tablespoons soy sauce
- 1 tablespoon sesame oil
- 1 egg, lightly beaten

How to cook:

Vegetable oil should be heated in a wok or big pan over high heat. Stir-fry the onion and garlic for 1-2 minutes, or until the onion and garlic release their aroma.

Stir-fry the shrimp for 2–3 minutes after you've peeled and deveined them, or until they turn pink and are opaque throughout.

Stir-fry for a further minute or two to heat through the defrosted peas and carrots.

Toss the beaten egg to one side of the pan and move the shrimp and veggies to the other. The egg must be scrambled until it is fully cooked.

Combine the scrambled egg with the shrimp and veggies in a mixing bowl.

Cooked white rice should be added to the pan and mixed together.

After the rice has been stir-fried for 1-2 minutes, pour the soy sauce and sesame oil over it to ensure that the rice is evenly covered and cooked.

Put in as much salt and pepper as you want.

A hot dish is what you need.

Nutrients:

Calories: 400

Fat: 16g

Carbohydrates: 45g

Protein: 20g

11. Beef Chow Fun

Items used:

- 8 oz wide rice noodles
- 1/2 lb flank steak, thinly sliced against the grain
- 2 cups bok choy, chopped
- 1 cup bean sprouts
- 2 cloves garlic, minced
- 2 tablespoons vegetable oil
- 2 tablespoons soy sauce
- 1 tablespoon oyster sauce
- Salt and pepper to taste

How to cook:

Prepare the wide rice noodles as directed on the box. Drain and put away.

Vegetable oil should be heated over high heat in a wok or big pan. Stir-fry the garlic mince for a minute or two, or until fragrant.

Stir-fry the flank steak for three to four minutes, or until it is browned and cooked through.

Chopped bok choy should be added to the skillet and stir-fried for an additional 2 minutes. Mix everything together for two to three minutes, or until soft.

Put in the rice noodles and mix everything together.

Stir-fry the noodles and veggies for a further minute or two just to make sure the noodles are cooked through and covered with the sauce.

Put in as much salt and pepper as you want.

A hot dish is what you need.

Nutrients:

Calories: 400

Fat: 12g

Carbohydrates: 50g

Protein: 20g

12. Vegetable Fried Rice

Items used:

- 8 oz cooked white rice, preferably leftover and chilled
- 1 cup mixed vegetables (carrots, peas, mushrooms), chopped
- 2 cloves garlic, minced
- 2 tablespoons vegetable oil
- 2 tablespoons soy sauce
- 1 tablespoon sesame oil
- 1 egg, lightly beaten

How to cook:

Table oil should be over high heat heated over high heat in a wok or big pan. Stir-fry the garlic mince for a minute or two, or until fragrant.

To cook the chopped veggies, add them to the skillet and stir-fry for two to three minutes, or until they are soft.

Toss the beaten egg into the empty half of the pan and push the veggies to one side. The egg must be scrambled until it is fully cooked.

Scramble the eggs and add them to the veggies.

Cooked white rice should be added to the pan and mixed together.

Once the rice and veggies have been stir-fried for 1-2 minutes, pour the soy sauce and sesame oil over the top.

Put in as much salt and pepper as you want.

A hot dish is what you need.

Nutrients:

Calories: 300

Fat: 12g

Carbohydrates: 40g

Protein: 8g

13. Cold Sesame Noodles

Items used:

- 8 oz thin noodles, cooked and chilled
- 1/4 cup sesame paste
- 2 tablespoons soy sauce
- 2 tablespoons Chinese black vinegar
- 1 tablespoon sesame oil
- 2 cloves garlic, minced
- 1 tablespoon sugar
- 1 tablespoon chili oil
- 2 scallions, thinly sliced

How to cook:

Prepare the thin noodles as directed on the packet. Drain the water and cool it down by rinsing it under cold water.

Combine the soy sauce, Chinese black vinegar, sesame oil, garlic, sugar, and chili oil in a small bowl and whisk until smooth.

Mix the sesame sauce with the cold noodles until they are uniformly covered.

Sprinkle with chopped scallions for presentation.

Eat chilled.

Nutrients:

Calories: 400

Fat: 16g

Carbohydrates: 50g

Protein: 12g

14. Pineapple Fried Rice

Items used:

- 8 oz cooked white rice, preferably leftover and chilled
- 1/2 lb shrimp or chicken, peeled and deveined or diced
- 1 cup pineapple chunks, fresh or canned
- 1/2 cup diced onion
- 1/2 cup diced red bell pepper
- 2 cloves garlic, minced
- 2 tablespoons vegetable oil
- 2 tablespoons soy sauce
- 1 tablespoon fish sauce
- 1 tablespoon curry powder
- Salt and pepper to taste

How to cook:

Vegetable oil should be heated over high heat in a wok or big pan. Stir-fry the garlic mince for a minute or two, or until fragrant.

Stir-fry the shrimp or chicken for 3–4 minutes, or until the shrimp or chicken is golden and cooked through.

Stir-fry for another 2–3 minutes, or until the onion and red bell pepper are cooked, if you've diced them.

Put the pineapple pieces in the pan and mix everything together.

Cooked white rice should be added to the pan and mixed together.

Once the rice and veggies have been stir-fried for 1-2 minutes, pour the soy sauce, fish sauce, and curry powder over the top.

Put in as much salt and pepper as you want.

A hot dish is what you need.

Nutrients:

Calories: 400

Fat: 12g

Carbohydrates: 50g

Protein: 20g

15. Garlic Noodles

Items used:

- 8 oz fresh egg noodles
- 4 cloves garlic, minced
- 2 tablespoons vegetable oil
- 2 tablespoons soy sauce
- 2 scallions, thinly sliced
- 1 tablespoon sesame seeds

How to cook:

Prepare the fresh egg noodles as directed on the box. Drain and put away.

In a large pan, melt the vegetable oil over moderate heat. Stir-fry the garlic mince for a minute or two, or until fragrant.

Cooked egg noodles should be added to the pan and mixed together.

After the noodles have been stir-fried for 1-2 minutes, pour the soy sauce over them and continue cooking to heat the sauce and coat the noodles.

Sprinkle with sesame seeds and top with thinly sliced scallions.

A hot dish is what you need.

Nutrients:

Calories: 400

Fat: 16g

Carbohydrates: 50g

Protein: 12g

CHAPTER 4

MEAT AND POULTRY

1. Kung Pao Chicken

Items used:

- 1 lb boneless, skinless chicken breasts, diced
- 1/2 cup roasted peanuts
- 2 tablespoons vegetable oil
- 2 cloves garlic, minced
- 1 tablespoon Sichuan peppercorns
- 2 dried red chilies
- 2 scallions, thinly sliced

For the marinade:

- 1 tablespoon cornstarch
- 1 tablespoon water
- 1 tablespoon white wine
- 1 tablespoon soy sauce

For the sauce:

- 2 tablespoons soy sauce
- 1 tablespoon Chinese black vinegar
- 1 tablespoon hoisin sauce
- 1 tablespoon honey
- 1 tablespoon cornstarch
- 1/4 cup water

How to cook:

Marinade may be made by combining cornstarch, water, white wine, and soy sauce in a small basin and whisking until smooth.

Coat the chicken cubes with the marinade and add them to the bowl. Marinate for at least 15 minutes.

Soy sauce, Chinese black vinegar, hoisin sauce, honey, cornstarch, and water should be whisked together in a separate small basin.

Vegetable oil should be heated in a wok or big pan over high heat. To create a fragrant stir-fry, add the garlic that has been minced, Sichuan peppercorns, and dried red chilies and cook for 1 to 2 minutes.

Stir-fry the chicken that has been marinated till it is browned and cooked through.

After the sauce has reduced and the chicken is covered, stir-fry for another minute or two.

Roasted peanuts should be added to the pan and mixed.

Sprinkle with chopped scallions for presentation.

A hot dish is what you need.

Nutrients:

Calories: 400

Fat: 16g

Carbohydrates: 20g

Protein: 40g

2. Mongolian Beef

Items used:

- 1 lb thinly sliced flank steak
- 1/4 cup cornstarch
- 1/4 cup vegetable oil
- 2 cloves garlic, minced
- 1 tablespoon minced fresh ginger
- 1/4 cup low-sodium soy sauce
- 1/3 cup water
- 1/2 cup packed brown sugar
- 4 sliced green onions
- Butter lettuce, for serving

How to cook:

One tablespoon of vegetable oil should be heated in a small saucepan over medium heat. Two minutes later, when the garlic and ginger are aromatic, add them. Dissolve the brown sugar in the water and soy sauce by stirring. Simmer for 10–12 minutes, uncovered, until reduced by half from boiling.

However, heat the remaining 1/4 cup of vegetable oil in a big pan over medium heat.

Cornstarch should be used to coat the flank steak in a big basin. The steak should be seared for 3–4 minutes in a hot pan.

Fat has to be drained.

After the sauce has simmered for a few minutes, add the green onion quarters and toss to mix.

Steak, topped with chopped green onions, served in lettuce cups.

Nutrients:

Calories: 400

Fat: 16g

Carbohydrates: 30g

Protein: 30g

3. Orange Chicken

Items used:

- 1 lb boneless chicken breasts
- 1/4 cup cornstarch
- 1/4 teaspoon salt
- 1/4 teaspoon black pepper
- 2 tablespoons vegetable oil
- 1/2 cup orange juice
- 1/4 cup brown sugar
- 1/4 cup rice vinegar
- 2 tablespoons soy sauce
- 1 tablespoon minced garlic
- 1 tablespoon minced ginger
- 1 tablespoon sesame oil
- 1 tablespoon orange zest
- 2 scallions, thinly sliced

How to cook:

Coat the chicken with cornstarch, salt, and pepper by tossing it around in a big basin.

In a large pan, melt the vegetable oil over moderate heat. To get a golden, crisp exterior on the chicken, frying it for 3–4 minutes on each side is required.

Combine the orange juice, sugar, and salt in a small saucepan. Stir in the rice vinegar, soy sauce, garlic, ginger, sesame oil, and brown sugar until the sugar is dissolved.

Simmer for 5-7 minutes, uncovered, until sauce has reduced and thickened.

Toss the crispy chicken pieces in the orange sauce to coat.

Orange zest and paper-thin scallion slices make a lovely garnish.

A hot dish is what you need.

Nutrients:

Calories: 400

Fat: 16g

Carbohydrates: 30g

Protein: 30g

4. Thai Basil Chicken

Items used:

- 1 lb minced chicken
- 2 tablespoons vegetable oil
- 3 cloves garlic, minced
- 2 shallots, thinly sliced
- 1 red Thai chili pepper, thinly sliced
- 1 cup Thai basil leaves
- 2 tablespoons fish sauce
- 1 tablespoon soy sauce
- 1 tablespoon oyster sauce
- 1 teaspoon sugar

How to cook:

Vegetable oil should be heated in a wok or big pan over high heat. Stir-fry the garlic, shallots, and red Thai chili pepper for 1-2 minutes, or until the garlic is aromatic.

Stir-fry the chicken mince for three to four minutes, or until it is browned and cooked.

After 1-2 minutes of stir-frying, pour the fish, soy, oyster, and sugar over the chicken to coat.

The Thai basil leaves should be added to the pan and mixed.

Eat with steaming hot rice.

Nutrients:

Calories: 400

Fat: 16g

Carbohydrates: 10g

Protein: 30g

5. Garlic Ginger Pork

Items used:

- 1 pound of boneless pork chops, cut crosswise into thin strips (approximately 1/4 inch thick).
- 2 tablespoons vegetable oil, divided
- 4 cloves garlic, minced
- 1 tablespoon grated fresh ginger
- 2 tablespoons soy sauce

How to cook:

Heat 1 tablespoon of vegetable oil over high heat in a large skillet. Cook the pork in a wok for three to four minutes, or until an instant-read thermometer registers 165 degrees.

The pork should be taken out of the pan and placed aside.

Over medium heat, warm the same skillet with the extra tablespoon of vegetable oil. Stir-fry the ginger and garlic for 1-2 minutes, or until the garlic is aromatic.

Return the pork after being cooked and pour the soy sauce into the pan. To ensure the pork is evenly covered in the sauce, stir-fry for another minute or two.

Eat with steaming hot rice.

Nutrients:

Calories: 400

Fat: 16g

Carbohydrates: 5g

Protein: 30g

6. Sizzling Steak Fajitas

Items used:

- 1 lb skirt steak, trimmed
- 1/4 cup vegetable oil
- 1/4 cup lime juice
- 2 tablespoons soy sauce
- 1 teaspoon chili powder
- 1/2 teaspoon ground cumin
- 1/2 teaspoon dried oregano
- 1/4 teaspoon salt
- 1/4 teaspoon black pepper
- 1 red bell pepper, sliced
- 1 green bell pepper, sliced
- 1 onion, sliced
- Flour tortillas, for serving
- Sour cream, for serving
- Guacamole, for serving
- Shredded cheese, for serving

How to cook:

Vegetable oil, lime juice, soy sauce, chili powder, powdered cumin, dried oregano, salt, black pepper, and a pinch of cayenne pepper should be mixed in a big bowl.

Toss the skirt steak in the basin to coat. Marinate for at least half an hour before serving.

Get a large skillet sizzling hot under high heat.

For about three to four minutes, till the peppers and onions have softened and begun to brown in the stir-fry, sauté the sliced ingredients. Discard the water and set the vegetables aside.

Marinated skirt steak needs three to four minutes in a hot wok to get desired browning and doneness.

Add the veggies to the pan with the meat when they cook.

Flour tortillas, guacamole, sour cream, and shredded cheese are great accompaniments.

Nutrients:

Calories: 400

Fat: 20g

Carbohydrates: 20g

Protein: 30g

7. Honey Sesame Chicken

Items used:

- 1 lb boneless chicken breasts
- 2 teaspoons minced garlic
- 1/4 cup cornstarch
- 2 teaspoons sesame seeds
- 2 teaspoons toasted sesame oil
- 1 tablespoon soy sauce
- 1 tablespoon sriracha
- 1/4 cup honey
- 1 tablespoon rice vinegar
- 1/4 cup water
- 2 tablespoons vegetable oil

How to cook:

To make the sauce, put the garlic that has been minced, cornstarch, sesame seeds, sesame oil, soy sauce, sriracha, honey, rice vinegar, and water in a deep bowl and whisk until smooth.

The chicken should be added to the dish and coated before being served.

In a large pan, melt the vegetable oil over moderate heat. Toss the chicken in the pan and fry until the chicken is golden and crispy.

Coat the chicken with the honey sesame sauce and set aside.

Eat with steaming hot rice.

Nutrients:

Calories: 400

Fat: 16g

Carbohydrates: 30g

Protein: 30g

8. Korean BBQ Beef

Items used:

- 1 lb beef tenderloin, cut into thin slices
- 1/4 cup soy sauce
- 2 tablespoons brown sugar
- 2 tablespoons sesame oil
- 2 tablespoons rice vinegar
- 2 cloves garlic, minced
- 1 tablespoon grated ginger
- 1/4 teaspoon black pepper
- 1/4 cup chopped scallions

How to cook:

Mix the soy sauce, brown sugar, sesame oil, rice vinegar, garlic, ginger, black pepper, and chopped garlic in a large bowl.

The meat should be cut and added to the basin to be coated. Marinate for at least half an hour before serving.

Prepare a high heat in a big skillet. Stir-fry the marinated meat for 3–4 minutes until browned and cooked through.

Serve hot over steaming rice and top with sliced scallions.

Nutrients:

Calories: 400

Fat: 20g

Carbohydrates: 10g

Protein: 30g

9. Spicy Sichuan Beef

Items used:

- 1 lb beef sirloin, sliced thinly against the grain
- 2 tablespoons cornstarch
- 2 tablespoons vegetable oil
- 1 red bell pepper, sliced
- 1 onion, sliced
- 2 cloves garlic, minced
- 1 tablespoon grated ginger
- 1 tablespoon Sichuan peppercorns
- 1 tablespoon soy sauce
- 1 tablespoon rice vinegar
- 1 tablespoon chili paste
- 1/4 cup chopped scallions

How to cook:

Coat the beef slices with cornstarch by tossing them in a large basin.

Vegetable oil should be heated over high heat in a big pan. In a pan, brown and crisp the meat in a stir-fry for 3 to 4 minutes. The steak should be removed from the pan and set aside.

Sliced bell peppers and onions should be stir-fried in the same pan for about three to four minutes, or until they are tender and starting to brown.

Stir-fry the garlic, ginger, and Sichuan peppercorns for 1-2 minutes, or until the garlic is golden and the ginger is aromatic.

Mix the soy sauce, rice vinegar, and chili paste in a small basin.

Put the meat back in the pan with the veggies when cooked, and then pour the sauce on top. Toss to blend, then cook for another minute or two to heat everything.

Serve hot over steaming rice and top with sliced scallions.

Nutrients:

Calories: 400

Fat: 20g

Carbohydrates: 20g

Protein: 30g

10. Cantonese-style Roast Duck

Items used:

- 1 whole duck, about 4-5 pounds
- 1/4 cup maltose syrup or honey
- 1 tablespoon rice vinegar
- 1/2 teaspoon red food coloring (optional)
- 1 cup warm water
- 1 tablespoon Chinese five-spice powder
- 1 tablespoon salt
- 1 tablespoon Shaoxing wine
- 1 tablespoon soy sauce
- 1 tablespoon hoisin sauce
- 1 tablespoon oyster sauce
- 1 tablespoon sesame oil
- 2 cloves garlic, minced
- 1 piece ginger, sliced
- 2 scallions, sliced

How to cook:

Put in a preheated 375°F oven.

Duck should be washed well and dried thoroughly using paper towels.

Mix the maltose syrup (or honey), rice vinegar, red food coloring (if using), and warm water in a small bowl with a whisk until well blended.

Combine the salt and Chinese five-spice powder in a separate, smaller bowl.

Coat the duck with the spice rub on both sides.

Carefully coat the duck with the maltose syrup mixture.

Mix the Shaoxing wine, soy sauce, hoisin sauce, oyster sauce, sesame oil, garlic, ginger, and scallions in a small bowl.

Put the sauce into the duck's cavity and then close it with needle and thread.

Roast the duck for 1 1/2 to 2 hours, basting every 20 minutes with the pan juices, after placing it on a rack in a roasting pan.

Roast for 10–15 minutes at 425°F, until the skin is golden and crispy.

Please wait 10 to 15 minutes after taking the duck out of the oven before attempting to carve it.

Serve immediately over hot, steaming rice with a sweet and sour sauce.

Nutrients:

Calories: 400

Fat: 20g

Carbohydrates: 10g

Protein: 30g

11. Hunan-style Spicy Pork

Items used:

- 1 lb pork tenderloin, sliced thinly
- 2 tablespoons soy sauce
- 2 tablespoons Shaoxing wine

- 1 tablespoon cornstarch
- 1 tablespoon vegetable oil
- 1 red bell pepper, sliced
- 1 onion, sliced
- 2 cloves garlic, minced
- 1 tablespoon grated ginger
- 2-3 dried chili peppers
- 1 tablespoon hoisin sauce
- 1 tablespoon oyster sauce
- 1 tablespoon sesame oil
- 1/4 cup chopped scallions

How to cook:

Soy sauce, Shaoxing wine, and cornstarch should be mixed in a large basin using a whisk.

Slice up some pork and put it in the bowl to coat it. Marinate for at least half an hour before serving.

Vegetable oil should be heated over high heat in a big pan. Stir-fry the pork, which has been marinated, for 3 to 4 minutes, or until it is browned and cooked through. The pork should be taken out of the pan and placed aside.

Sliced bell peppers and onions should be stir-fried in the same pan for about three to four minutes, or until they are tender and starting to brown.

Stir-fry the garlic, ginger, and dried chilies for 1-2 minutes, or until the garlic and ginger are aromatic.

Mix 1/4 cup water, the oyster sauce, the hoisin sauce, Whisk together the water, sesame oil, and a small bowl.

Pour the sauce over the pork and veggies once you return the cooked meat to the pan. Toss to blend, then cook for another minute or two to heat everything.

Serve hot over steaming rice and top with sliced scallions.

Nutrients:

Calories: 400

Fat: 20g

Carbohydrates: 10g

Protein: 30g

12. Lemon Pepper Chicken

Items used:

- 4 boneless, skinless chicken breasts
- 2 tablespoons lemon juice
- 1/4 teaspoon ground black pepper
- 1/4 teaspoon garlic powder
- 1/4 teaspoon salt
- 1 tablespoon olive oil

How to cook:

Put in a preheated 375°F oven.

Black pepper, garlic powder, and salt may be added to the lemon juice in a small dish and whisked together.

Coat the chicken breasts equally with the lime juice mixture and place them in a baking dish.

Spread the chicken breasts with the olive oil.

Chicken should be baked for 25-30 minutes until it's no longer pinkish in the middle.

After 5 minutes in the oven, take the chicken out and allow it rest before cutting and serving.

Nutrients:

Calories: 200

Fat: 5g

Carbohydrates: 2g

Protein: 35g

13. Vietnamese Lemongrass Beef

Items used:

- 1 lb beef sirloin, sliced thinly
- 2 tablespoons lemongrass, minced
- 2 cloves garlic, minced
- 2 tablespoons fish sauce
- 2 tablespoons brown sugar
- 1 tablespoon vegetable oil
- 1/4 cup chopped scallions

How to cook:

Combine the lemongrass, garlic, fish sauce, and brown sugar in a deep bowl using a whisk.

The meat should be cut and added to the basin to be coated. Marinate for at least half an hour before serving.

Vegetable oil should be heated over high heat in a big pan. Stir-fry the marinated meat for 3–4 minutes until browned and cooked through.

Remove the meat from the heat and let it to rest for a while.

Serve hot over steaming rice and top with sliced scallions.

Nutrients:

Calories: 400

Fat: 20g

Carbohydrates: 10g

Protein: 30g

14. Five-spice Beef and Broccoli

Items used:

- 1 lb beef sirloin, sliced thinly

- 1 bunch broccoli, cut into florets
- 2 tablespoons soy sauce
- 1 tablespoon Chinese five-spice powder
- 1 tablespoon vegetable oil
- 1/4 cup chopped scallions

How to cook:

Soy sauce and Chinese five spice powder should be mixed in a large bowl using a whisk.

The meat should be cut and added to the basin to be coated. Marinate for at least half an hour before serving.

Vegetable oil should be heated over high heat in a big pan. Stir-fry the marinated meat for 3–4 minutes, until it's browned and cooked.

Remove the meat from the heat and let it to rest for a while.

Then, stir-fry the broccoli florets in the same pan for three to four minutes, or until they are brilliant green and soft.

Stir the cooked meat and broccoli back into the pan they were cooked in.

Serve hot over steaming rice and top with sliced scallions.

Nutrients:

Calories: 400

Fat: 20g

Carbohydrates: 10g

Protein: 30g

15. Japanese Teriyaki Chicken

Items used:

- 1 lb boneless, skinless chicken breasts, sliced thinly
- 1/4 cup low-sodium soy sauce
- 1/4 cup sake

- 1/4 cup brown sugar
- 1 tablespoon rice vinegar
- 1 tablespoon vegetable oil
- 1 clove garlic, minced
- 1 teaspoon grated ginger

How to cook:

Mix the soy sauce, sake, brown sugar, rice vinegar, garlic, and ginger paste in a small bowl using a whisk.

Toss the chicken strips into the basin to coat. Marinade for at least half an hour before serving.

Vegetable oil should be heated over high heat in a big pan. Stir-fry the chicken with the marinade for three to four minutes, or until the chicken is browned and cooked.

Take the prepared chicken from the pan and put it to one side.

Bring the same skillet to a boil with the remaining marinade. Simmer on low for two to three minutes till the sauce has thickened.

Stir the thickened sauce back into the pan where the chicken was cooked.

Garnish with chopped scallions or sesame seeds and serve immediately over steaming rice.

Nutrients:

Calories: 400

Fat: 20g

Carbohydrates: 10g

Protein: 30g

CHAPTER 5

SEAFOOD

1. Shrimp Stir-Fry

Items used:

- 1 lb raw shrimp, peeled and deveined
- 1 red bell pepper, sliced
- 3 cups broccoli, chopped small
- 1 small bag snap peas
- 2 tablespoons avocado oil
- 2 cloves garlic, minced
- 1 tablespoon grated ginger
- 1/4 cup low-sodium soy sauce
- 1 tablespoon honey
- 1 tablespoon cornstarch
- 1/4 cup chopped scallions

How to cook:

Mix the soy sauce, honey, and cornstarch in a deep bowl using a whisk.

In a large pan, melt the avocado oil over high heat. Stir-fry the sliced bell pepper, chopped broccoli, and snap peas for 3–4 minutes, or until the vegetables are just beginning to soften.

Stir-fry the ginger and garlic for 1-2 minutes, or until the garlic is golden and the ginger is aromatic.

Stir-fry the raw shrimp for three to four minutes until they become pink and are fully cooked.

Toss the shrimp and veggies in the soy sauce mixture and mix well. Continue cooking for two to three minutes to thicken the sauce.

Serve hot over steaming rice and top with sliced scallions.

Nutrients:

Calories: 300

Fat: 10g

Carbohydrates: 20g

Protein: 30g

2. Singapore Chili Crab

Items used:

- 2 lbs whole crabs, cleaned and cracked
- 1/4 cup chili sauce
- 1/4 cup tomato sauce
- 2 tablespoons vegetable oil
- 2 cloves garlic, minced
- 1 tablespoon grated ginger
- 1 tablespoon cornstarch
- 2 tablespoons water
- 1/4 cup chopped scallions

How to cook:

Combine the tomato sauce, chili sauce, cornstarch, and water in a deep bowl and stir until smooth.

Vegetable oil should be heated over high heat in a big pan. Stir-fry the ginger and garlic for 1-2 minutes, or until the garlic is golden and the ginger is aromatic.

Stir-fry the crabs for 3–4 minutes, or until they have a light brown color and a meaty texture.

Toss the crabs with the chili sauce mixture and serve. Continue cooking for another 5–7 minutes until the crabs are done and the sauce thickens.

Serve hot over steaming rice and top with sliced scallions.

Nutrients:

Calories: 300

Fat: 10g

Carbohydrates: 20g

Protein: 30g

3. Thai Green Curry with Seafood

Items used:

- 1/2 lb shrimp, peeled and deveined
- 1/2 lb squid, cleaned and sliced into rings
- 1/2 lb mussels, cleaned and debearded
- 1/4 cup green curry paste
- 1 can (14 oz) coconut milk
- 1 tablespoon vegetable oil
- 1 tablespoon grated ginger
- 1 tablespoon minced lemongrass
- 1 tablespoon fish sauce
- 1 tablespoon brown sugar
- 1/4 cup chopped cilantro

How to cook:

In a large pan, melt the vegetable oil over moderate heat. Stir-fry the minced lemongrass and grated ginger for a minute or two until aromatic.

Green curry paste should be added to the skillet and mixed.

Once the pan is hot, add the rinsed and prepped seafood and stir-frying for 3 to 4 minutes.

Add the coconut milk and mix it in with the fish. Fish sauce and brown sugar should be stirred in at this point.

Repeat steps 5-7 until the sauce thickens and the seafood is cooked.

Serve hot with steaming rice and garnish with chopped cilantro.

Nutrients:

Calories: 400

Fat: 20g

Carbohydrates: 10g

Protein: 30g

4. Clams in Black Bean Sauce

Items used:

- 3 dozen medium fresh clams, in the shell
- 1/4 cup cornmeal
- 1 1/2 tablespoons salt
- 1/2 cup vegetable oil
- 3 slices fresh ginger, julienned
- 3 cloves garlic, minced
- 1 tablespoon fermented black beans
- 1 tablespoon cornstarch
- 2 tablespoons water
- Chopped scallions for garnish

How to cook:

Mix the cornmeal and salt in a big basin. Put the clams in a bowl and cover them with water. Give it half an hour to soak.

The clams should be drained and washed in cold water. Cracked or open clams should be thrown away.

Vegetable oil should be heated over high heat in a big pan—Stir-fry the julienned ginger and minced garlic for 1 to 2 minutes, or until fragrant.

The fermented black beans should be added to the pan and mixed well.

Put the clams in the pan and stir-fry for about 4 minutes, or until they start to brown.

Cornstarch and water should be mixed well in a small bowl. Toss the clams with the cornstarch mixture and whisk to incorporate. Continue cooking for two to three minutes to thicken the sauce.

Serve immediately when hot, garnished with sliced scallions.

Nutrients:

Calories: 200

Fat: 10g

Carbohydrates: 10g

Protein: 20g

5. Steamed Fish with Ginger and Scallions

Items used:

- 1 lb fresh fish fillets (such as cod or snapper)
- 2 tablespoons soy sauce
- 2 tablespoons rice vinegar
- 1 tablespoon grated ginger
- 2 scallions, thinly sliced
- 1 tablespoon vegetable oil

- Salt and pepper to taste

How to cook:

Fish fillets should be washed and dried with paper towels before cooking. Put in as much salt and pepper as you want.

To make the sauce, combine the soy sauce, rice vinegar, ginger, and scallions in a small bowl and whisk until well combined.

Prepare a heat-safe plate that can fit inside a steamer basket for the fish fillets. The fish fillets should be soaked in the soy sauce mixture.

Bring approximately two inches of water to a boil in a big saucepan or wok. Cover the steamer basket with the lid and set it over the pot of boiling water.

The fish fillets need 8-10 minutes in the steamer to get an ideal flaky texture.

Carefully lift the steamer basket with the fish fillets from the saucepan or wok.

Fish fillets may be topped with a drizzle of vegetable oil and some sliced scallions for presentation.

Nutrients:

Calories: 200

Fat: 6g

Carbohydrates: 4g

Protein: 30g

6. Seafood Pad Thai

Items used:

- 1/2 lb pad Thai rice noodles
- 1/2 lb shrimp, peeled and deveined
- 1/2 lb squid, cleaned and sliced into rings
- 2 eggs, beaten
- 1/4 cup fish sauce

- 2 tablespoons tamarind paste

- 2 tablespoons brown sugar

- 2 tablespoons vegetable oil

- 2 cloves garlic, minced

- 1/4 cup chopped scallions

- 1/4 cup chopped peanuts

- 1 lime, cut into wedges

How to cook:

Rice noodles must be softened by soaking in warm water for 30 minutes. Drain and put away.

Mix the fish sauce, tamarind paste, and brown sugar in a deep bowl and whisk to mix.

Vegetable oil should be heated over high heat in a big pan. Stir-fry the minced garlic for a minute or two, or until fragrant, until it is added to the pan.

Stir-fry the shrimp and squid for 3–4 minutes, or until they begin to color.

Move the shrimp and squid to one side of the pan to make room for the eggs. The eggs need to be scrambled until they are done.

The rice noodles should be softened before being added to the pan. Toss the noodles with the sauce made from fish and sugar.

Noodles should be cooked through and the sauce should have thickened after another 5–7 minutes of cooking.

Decorate with peanuts, scallions, and lime wedges.

Nutrients:

Calories: 400

Fat: 15g

Carbohydrates: 50g

Protein: 20g

7. Salt and Pepper Squid

Items used:

- 1 lb squid, cleaned and sliced into rings
- 1/2 cup cornstarch
- 1 teaspoon salt
- 1 teaspoon black pepper
- 1-2 chili peppers, thinly sliced
- Vegetable oil for frying

How to cook:

Cornstarch, salt, and black pepper should all be mixed in a big basin. Throw in the sliced squid and stir to cover everything well.

Vegetable oil should be heated over high heat in a big pan or wok. Stir-fry the coated squid for 3–4 minutes, or until the coating is crispy and the squid is golden brown.

The squid may be drained of excess oil by placing it on a dish lined with paper towels after being removed from the pan using a slotted spoon.

Thinly slice the Chile peppers and add them, along with a sprinkling of salt, to a small bowl.

Toss the fried squid with the chili pepper mixture to coat.

Whether as an appetizer or a snack, serve hot.

Nutrients:

Calories: 200

Fat: 10g

Carbohydrates: 15g

Protein: 15g

8. Szechuan Shrimp

Items used:

- 1 lb shrimp, peeled and deveined

- 1/2 cup cornstarch

- Salt and pepper to taste

- 2 tablespoons vegetable oil

- 8 cloves garlic, minced

- 1 tablespoon grated ginger

- 2-3 dried chili peppers, chopped

- 1 tablespoon Szechuan peppercorns

- 1/4 cup soy sauce

- 1 tablespoon rice vinegar

- 1 tablespoon brown sugar

- 1 tablespoon sesame oil

How to cook:

Cornstarch, salt, and black pepper should all be mixed together in a big basin. Throw in the sliced squid and stir to cover everything well.

Vegetable oil should be heated over high heat in a big pan or wok. Stir-fry the coated squid for 3–4 minutes, or until the coating is crispy and the squid is golden brown.

The squid may be drained of excess oil by placing it on a dish lined with paper towels after being removed from the pan using a slotted spoon.

Thinly slice the Chile peppers and add them, along with a sprinkling of salt, to a small bowl.

Toss the fried squid with the chili pepper mixture to coat.

Whether as an appetizer or a snack, serve hot.

Nutrients:

Calories: 300

Fat: 10g

Carbohydrates: 20g

Protein: 30g

9. Crab Rangoon

Items used:

- 5 oz canned crab meat, drained and flaked
- 4 oz cream cheese, softened
- 1 green onion, finely sliced
- 1 clove garlic, minced
- 1 teaspoon Worcestershire sauce
- Salt and pepper to taste
- 20 wonton wrappers
- Vegetable oil for frying

How to cook:

Drain the crab meat and flake it into small pieces. Cream cheese, green onion, garlic, Worcestershire sauce, Pepper and salt should be combined in one large bowl.

Incorporate all ingredients by mixing well.

Spread out the wonton wrappers so they may be used. Fill the middle of each wonton wrapper with the crab filling.

Run water down the edges of the wonton wrapper with your fingertips. The wonton wrapper is made by folding the square into a triangle and then pressing the three points together.

Vegetable oil should be heated over high heat in a big pan or wok. Put the wontons in the pan and cook for two or three minutes, or until they are golden and crispy.

With a slotted spoon, transfer the fried wontons from the pan to a dish lined with paper towels to soak up any leftover oil.

Dip with sweet and sour or soy sauce while still hot.

Nutrients:

Calories: 150

Fat: 8g

Carbohydrates: 15g

Protein: 5g

10. Lobster with Ginger and Scallions

Items used:

- 2 lobsters, about 1 1/2 lbs each
- 2 tablespoons vegetable oil
- 2 tablespoons grated ginger
- 2 scallions, thinly sliced
- 2 cloves garlic, minced
- 1 tablespoon soy sauce
- 1 tablespoon rice vinegar
- 1 tablespoon brown sugar
- Salt and pepper to taste

How to cook:

Put some salt into a big kettle of water and get it boiling. Cook the lobsters for 8-10 minutes, or until the flesh is tender and the shells are a deep, crimson color.

Take the lobsters away from the heat for a while so they can chill off. Separate the flesh from the shells of the claws and tails. Piece the meat up so it's easy to consume.

Vegetable oil should be heated over high heat in a big pan or wok. Stir-fry the grated ginger, ginger, thinly sliced scallions, and minced garlic for 1-2 minutes, or until the scallions and ginger release their scent.

The lobster flesh should be added to the pan after it has been cooked. Toss the lobster flesh with the soy sauce, rice vinegar, and brown sugar.

Continue cooking for another 2–3 minutes, or until the lobster is cooked through and well covered with the sauce.

Eat with steaming hot rice.

Nutrients:

Calories: 300

Fat: 10g

Carbohydrates: 10g

Protein: 40g

11. Spicy Garlic Scallop Stir-Fry

Items used:

- 1 lb scallops, cleaned
- 2 tablespoons vegetable oil
- 4 cloves garlic, minced
- 1-2 chili peppers, thinly sliced
- 2 tablespoons soy sauce
- 1 tablespoon rice vinegar
- 1 tablespoon brown sugar
- Salt and pepper to taste

How to cook:

Vegetable oil should be heated over high heat in a big pan or wok. To create a fragrant stir-fry, add the minced garlic and thinly sliced Chile peppers to the pan and cook for 1 to 2 minutes.

Put the cleaned scallops in the pan and stir-fry for two to three minutes, or until they are just opaque throughout and beginning to brown.

Soy sauce, rice vinegar, brown sugar, salt, and pepper should be combined in a small basin and whisked together.

Add the sauce to the scallops in the pan and mix well. Hold off on serving the scallops until the sauce has thickened enough to coat them, usually another minute or two in the oven.

Eat with steaming hot rice.

Nutrients:

Calories: 200

Fat: 8g

Carbohydrates: 10g

Protein: 20g

12. Chinese-style Steamed Mussels

Items used:

- 2 lbs fresh mussels
- 2 tablespoons vegetable oil
- 2 cloves garlic, minced
- 1 tablespoon grated ginger
- 1 tablespoon fermented black beans, rinsed and mashed
- 1/4 cup Chinese rice wine or dry sherry
- 2 tablespoons soy sauce
- 1 tablespoon sesame oil
- 2 scallions, thinly sliced

How to cook:

Vegetable oil should be heated over medium heat in a big pan or wok. Stir-fry the fermented black beans, ginger, and garlic for 1-2 minutes, or until the garlic and ginger are aromatic.

After the mussels have been cleaned, add them to the pan and toss them in the garlic and ginger mixture.

Cover the pan with the lid and add the Chinese rice wine or dry sherry to the mussels. Cook the mussels for 7-10 minutes in boiling water until the shells have opened.

Stir the soy sauce and sesame oil together in a small bowl.

Take the cooked mussels out of the pan and transfer them to a large serving dish. Toss the mussels in the soy sauce and sesame oil mixture to coat.

Serve immediately with thinly sliced scallions as a garnish.

Nutrients:

Calories: 200

Fat: 8g

Carbohydrates: 8g

Protein: 20g

13. Stir-fried Squid with Vegetables

Items used:

- 1 lb squid, cut into rings
- 1 red bell pepper, thinly sliced
- 1 green bell pepper, thinly sliced
- 1 onion, thinly sliced
- 2 cloves garlic, minced
- 2 tablespoons vegetable oil
- 2 tablespoons soy sauce
- 1 tablespoon oyster sauce
- 1 tablespoon cornstarch
- Salt and pepper to taste

How to cook:

Mix the soy sauce, oyster sauce, cornstarch, salt, and pepper in a small basin.

Vegetable oil should be heated over high heat in a big pan or wok. Stir-fry the minced garlic for a minute or two, or until fragrant, until it is added to the pan.

Stir-fry the sliced bell peppers and onion for 2–3 minutes, or until they have softened somewhat.

Stir-fry the squid rings for 2–3 minutes, or until they are thoroughly cooked and tender.

Toss the squid and vegetables in the pan with the soy sauce and oyster sauce combination.

Cook for about a minute, or until the sauce has thickened and covered the squid and veggies.

Eat with steaming hot rice.

Nutrients:

Calories: 200

Fat: 8g

Carbohydrates: 15g

Protein: 20g

14. Cantonese-style Steamed Fish

Items used:

- 1 whole fresh fish, about 2 lbs (such as sea bass or red snapper), cleaned and scaled
- 2 tablespoons soy sauce
- 2 tablespoons Shaoxing wine or dry sherry
- 2 tablespoons vegetable oil
- 2 tablespoons grated ginger
- 2 scallions, thinly sliced
- Salt and pepper to taste

How to cook:

The entire fish should be rinsed after being scaled and cleaned, and then dried with paper towels. Before serving, season with salt and pepper to taste.

Mix the soy sauce and Shaoxing wine (or dry sherry) in a small bowl.

Cook the fish in a steamer by placing it on a heat-resistant plate. Rinse the fish and then cover it with the soy sauce, Shaoxing wine, or dry sherry combination.

Toss the salmon with the grated ginger and cut scallions.

Bring water for the steamer to a rolling boil. Cook the fish for 12-15 minutes in the steamer until it is thoroughly cooked and tender.

Warm the vegetable oil in a small saucepan over low heat. Toss the fish that has been steamed in the heated oil.

Eat with steaming hot rice.

Nutrients:

Calories: 200

Fat: 8g

Carbohydrates: 2g

Protein: 30g

15. Coconut Curry Shrimp

Items used:

- 1 lb shrimp, peeled and deveined
- 1 tablespoon curry paste
- 1 can (14 oz) coconut milk
- 1 red bell pepper, thinly sliced
- 1 onion, thinly sliced
- 2 cloves garlic, minced
- 1 tablespoon grated ginger
- 2 tablespoons vegetable oil
- Salt and pepper to taste

How to cook:

Mix the curry paste and coconut milk in a separate small bowl.

In a big pan or wok, melt the vegetable oil over moderate heat. Stir-fry the ginger and garlic for 1-2 minutes, or until the garlic is golden and the ginger is aromatic.

The red bell pepper and onion may be added to the pan and stir-fried for two to three minutes to soften.

Stir-fry the shrimp for 2–3 minutes after you've peeled and deveined them, or until they become pink.

Toss the shrimp and veggies in the pan with the curry paste and coconut milk combination.

Keep the shrimp and veggies in the pan for another minute or two so the sauce can thicken and coat them.

Eat with steaming hot rice.

Nutrients:

Calories: 250

Fat: 16g

Carbohydrates: 10g

Protein: 20g

CHAPTER 6

VEGETARIAN AND VEGAN

1. Vegan Pad Thai

Items used:

- 8 oz rice noodles

- 2 tablespoons vegetable oil

- 8 oz firm tofu, cut into 1/2" cubes

- 1 shallot, thinly sliced

- 3 cloves garlic, minced

- 1 red bell pepper, thinly sliced

- 1 carrot, peeled and julienned

- 1 cup bean sprouts

- 1/4 cup chopped peanuts

- 2 tablespoons chopped cilantro

- Lime wedges for serving

- For the sauce:

- 1/4 cup vegetable broth
- 1/4 cup soy sauce
- 2 tablespoons brown sugar
- 1 tablespoon tamarind paste
- 1 tablespoon rice vinegar
- 1 tablespoon sriracha

How to cook:

Rice noodles should be prepared in accordance with package directions. Drain and put away.

Vegetable broth, soy sauce, brown sugar, tamarind paste, rice vinegar, and sriracha are whisked together in a small dish to form the sauce.

Vegetable oil should be heated over high heat in a big pan or wok. Stir-fry the tofu cubes for two to three minutes, or until they are gently browned.

Wait for the sauce to thicken and coat the squid and veggies, about a minute and a half of cooking time.

Stir-fry the red bell pepper and julienned carrot for 2–3 minutes, or until the vegetables are just tender.

Cooked rice noodles and bean sprouts may be tossed together in the pan.

Stir the sauce into the pan of noodles and vegetables to coat.

Keep the noodles and veggies in the pan for another two minutes or until the sauce has thickened and covered everything.

Garnish with chopped peanuts and cilantro and a squeeze of fresh lime juice before serving.

Nutrients:

Calories: 400

Fat: 16g

Carbohydrates: 50g

Protein: 16g

2. Chinese-style Eggplant Stir-Fry

Items used:

- 2 medium eggplants, cut into bite-sized pieces
- 2 tablespoons vegetable oil
- 3 cloves garlic, minced
- 1 tablespoon grated ginger
- 2 tablespoons soy sauce
- 1 tablespoon rice vinegar
- 1 tablespoon brown sugar
- 1/4 cup vegetable broth
- 2 scallions, thinly sliced

How to cook:

Vegetable oil should be heated over high heat in a big pan or wok. Stir-fry the eggplant for two to three minutes, or until it has softened and browned slightly.

Stir-fry the ginger and garlic for 1-2 minutes, or until the garlic is golden and the ginger is aromatic.

To create the sauce, combine the soy sauce, rice vinegar, brown sugar, and vegetable broth in a small bowl and whisk until smooth.

When the eggplant has cooked for a few minutes, pour the sauce over it and mix to coat.

Cook for another minute or two, or until the eggplant is completely submerged in the sauce.

Serve hot over steaming rice and garnish with sliced scallions.

Nutrients:

Calories: 150

Fat: 8g

Carbohydrates: 20g

Protein: 3g

3. Szechuan-style Mapo Tofu

Items used:

- 14 oz soft tofu, drained and cut into small cubes
- 1 tablespoon vegetable oil
- 6 oz ground pork or beef
- 2 tablespoons spicy chili bean paste (doubanjiang)
- 1 tablespoon black beans, rinsed and chopped
- 1 tablespoon grated ginger
- 3 cloves garlic, minced
- 1/2 teaspoon ground Sichuan peppercorns
- 1/2 cup vegetable broth
- 2 tablespoons soy sauce
- 1 tablespoon cornstarch
- 2 tablespoons water
- 2 scallions, thinly sliced

How to cook:

Vegetable oil should be heated over high heat in a big pan or wok. Ground pork or beef should be added to the pan and stir-fried for 2 to 3 minutes.

Stir-fry the fermented black beans, ginger, garlic, and powdered Sichuan peppercorns for 1-2 minutes until aromatic, then add the spicy chili bean paste.

Stir the cubed tofu into the pan along with the ground pig or beef.

Whisk together the vegetable broth, soy sauce, water, and cornstarch in a small basin.

Toss the tofu and meat mixture in the pan with the slurry and swirl to combine.

Wait another minute or two for the sauce to thicken and cover the tofu and pork, then serve.

Serve hot over steaming rice and garnish with sliced scallions.

Nutrients:

Calories: 250

Fat: 16g

Carbohydrates: 10g

Protein: 18g

4. Thai Green Curry with Tofu and Vegetables

Items used:

- 1 package (14 oz) extra-firm tofu, drained and cut into bite-sized pieces
- 1 tablespoon coconut oil
- 1 yellow onion, sliced
- 1 tablespoon grated ginger
- 3 cloves garlic, minced
- 2 tablespoons green curry paste
- 1 can (13.5 oz) coconut milk
- 1 cup vegetable broth
- 1 red bell pepper, sliced
- 1 zucchini, sliced
- 1 cup green beans, trimmed
- 1 tablespoon soy sauce
- 1 tablespoon brown sugar
- 1 tablespoon lime juice
- Salt and pepper to taste
- Fresh cilantro for garnish

How to cook:

In a large pan or wok, melt the coconut oil over moderate heat. Stir-fry the sliced onion, grated ginger, and minced garlic for 1-2 minutes, or until the onion and ginger are soft and the garlic is fragrant.

Stir-fry for another minute or two after adding the green curry paste, or until aromatic.

Put the curry paste in a skillet and add the coconut milk and vegetable broth, stirring to combine.

Put the curry mixture in a pan and add the sliced red bell pepper, zucchini, and green beans.

Add the cubed tofu to the pan, along with the veggies and curry sauce, and stir gently to blend.

Season with salt, pepper, lime juice, brown sugar, and soy sauce.

Keep going for another 5–7 minutes until the veggies are soft and the tofu is warmed thoroughly.

Serve hot with steaming rice and garnish with fresh cilantro.

Nutrients:

Calories: 300

Fat: 20g

Carbohydrates: 20g

Protein: 12g

5. Vegetarian Kung Pao Tofu

Items used:

- 1 block (14-16 oz) extra-firm tofu, drained and cut into small cubes
- 2 tablespoons vegetable oil
- 1 red bell pepper, sliced
- 1 onion, chopped
- 2 cloves garlic, minced
- 1/4 cup peanuts
- 2 tablespoons soy sauce
- 1 tablespoon rice vinegar
- 1 tablespoon brown sugar
- 1 tablespoon cornstarch
- 1/4 cup vegetable broth
- 1 teaspoon sesame oil
- 1 teaspoon Sichuan peppercorns
- Salt and pepper to taste

How to cook:

Vegetable oil should be heated over high heat in a big pan or wok. Stir-fry the tofu cubes for two to three minutes, or until they are gently browned.

Stir-fry the sliced red bell pepper, chopped onion, and minced garlic for 2–3 minutes, or until the vegetables have softened somewhat.

Mix the soy sauce, rice vinegar, brown sugar, cornstarch, and vegetable broth together in a small basin.

Add the sauce to the pan, then toss in the tofu and vegetables.

The peanuts should be added to the skillet and mixed together.

The sauce should thicken and cover the tofu, veggies, and peanuts after another minute or two in the pan.

To taste, season with salt, pepper, and Sichuan peppercorns and drizzle with sesame oil.

Eat with steaming hot rice.

Nutrients:

Calories: 300

Fat: 20g

Carbohydrates: 15g

Protein: 18g

6. Stir-fried Bok Choy

Items used:

- 4 heads bok choy, washed and sliced
- 2 teaspoons sesame oil
- 1 teaspoon grated ginger
- 2 cloves garlic, minced
- 2 tablespoons reduced-sodium soy sauce
- Salt and black pepper to taste

How to cook:

In a large pan or wok, melt the sesame oil over moderate heat. Spruce up your pan with some freshly grated ginger and chopped garlic by cooking them together for a minute.

The leaves of the bok choy should be wilted and the stalks crisp-tender before you add them to the pan.

Add the soy sauce to the bok choy in the pan and toss to coat.

Black pepper and salt to taste.

Use as a topping for steaming rice or as a hot side dish.

Nutrients:

Calories: 50

Fat: 3g

Carbohydrates: 5g

Protein: 3g

7. Vegan Singapore Noodles

Items used:

- 8 oz rice vermicelli noodles
- 1 tablespoon vegetable oil
- 1 red bell pepper, julienned
- 1 yellow onion, sliced
- 2 cloves garlic, minced
- 1 tablespoon curry powder
- 1/2 teaspoon turmeric
- 1/4 teaspoon cayenne pepper
- 1/4 cup vegetable broth
- 2 tablespoons soy sauce
- 1 tablespoon brown sugar
- 1 cup bean sprouts

- 1/4 cup chopped scallions
- Lime wedges for serving

How to cook:

Rice vermicelli noodles should be prepared as directed on the box. Drain and put away.

Vegetable oil should be heated over high heat in a big pan or wok. Cook the julienned red bell pepper, sliced yellow onion, and minced garlic in a skillet over medium heat for about 2 to 3 minutes, or until the veggies have softened

Cook for another minute or two, or until the curry powder, turmeric, and cayenne pepper have released their scent.

In a deep bowl, combine the soy sauce, brown sugar, and vegetable broth.

Add the prepared sauce to the pan with the vegetables and toss to coat.

Cooked rice vermicelli noodles may be added to the pan and mixed with the sauce and vegetables.

Put the bean sprouts in the pan and mix everything together.

Continue cooking for another minute or two, or until the bean sprouts have softened somewhat.

Serve hot with lime wedges and garnish with chopped scallions.

Nutrients:

Calories: 250

Fat: 4g

Carbohydrates: 48g

Protein: 5g

8. Vegan Teriyaki Tofu Stir-Fry

Items used:

- 1 (14 oz) block firm tofu, drained and cubed
- 2 tablespoons cornstarch
- 1 tablespoon vegetable oil

- 1 red bell pepper, sliced
- 1 yellow onion, sliced
- 2 cloves garlic, minced
- 1/4 cup soy sauce
- 1/4 cup sake
- 2 tablespoons brown sugar
- 1 tablespoon cornstarch
- Salt and pepper to taste
- Cooked rice for serving

How to cook:

Cube the tofu and coat it with cornstarch (about 2 teaspoons).

Vegetable oil should be heated over high heat in a big pan or wok. To get the tofu crispy and golden brown, add it to the pan after it has been coated and stir-fry for 5 to 7 minutes.

The red bell pepper, yellow onion, and garlic should be added to the pan and stir-fried for about two minutes, or until the vegetables have softened somewhat.

To create the teriyaki sauce, combine the soy sauce, sake, brown sugar, and cornstarch in a small bowl and whisk until smooth.

Toss the tofu and vegetables in the pan with the teriyaki sauce and swirl to coat.

Keep the tofu and veggies in the pan for another minute or two so the sauce can thicken and cover everything.

Put in as much salt and pepper as you want.

Eat with hot cooked rice.

Nutrients:

Calories: 300

Fat: 10g

Carbohydrates: 30g

Protein: 20g

9. Thai Pineapple Fried Rice

Items used:

- 2 tablespoons vegetable oil
- 2 eggs, beaten with salt
- 1 1/2 cups chopped fresh pineapple
- 1 red bell pepper, diced
- 1 small onion, diced
- 2 cloves garlic, minced
- 1 small bird's eye chili, minced
- 4 cups cooked jasmine rice, chilled
- 1/2 cup roasted cashews
- 2 tablespoons soy sauce
- 1 tablespoon fish sauce (optional)
- 1 tablespoon brown sugar
- 1/4 cup chopped fresh cilantro
- Lime wedges for serving

How to cook:

Vegetable oil should be heated over high heat in a big pan or wok. Scramble and brown the eggs for 1-2 minutes in the skillet once they have been beaten. Take out of the frying pan.

Stir-fry the fresh pineapple, red bell pepper, onion, garlic, and bird's eye Chile for 2 to 3 minutes, or until the vegetables have softened somewhat.

Cooked jasmine rice should be added to the pan and mixed in with the pineapple and vegetables.

Stir in the brown sugar, soy sauce, fish sauce (if using), and roasted cashews to the pan.

Continue cooking for a further two to three minutes, or until the rice is hot and the flavors have blended.

Scramble the eggs and add the fresh cilantro that has been chopped.

Hot, with lime wedges on the side.

Nutrients:

Calories: 400

Fat: 15g

Carbohydrates: 60g

Protein: 10g

10. Vegan Miso Soup

Items used:

- 4 cups vegetable broth
- 1/2 cup sliced mushrooms
- 1/2 cup diced tofu
- 1/4 cup sliced scallions
- 2 tablespoons miso paste
- 1/4 cup sliced seaweed
- 1 tablespoon soy sauce
- 1 tablespoon rice vinegar
- 1 teaspoon grated ginger
- 1 clove garlic, minced

How to cook:

Bring the vegetable broth to a rolling boil in a saucepan by heating it over a high temperature.

Turn the flame down to medium and add some mushrooms, tofu, onions, and seaweed to the pan. After that, stir everything together.

Thoroughly mix the miso paste, soy sauce, rice vinegar, ginger, and garlic paste in a deep bowl. Mix until everything is incorporated.

Put the miso sauce in the saucepan and mix it well.

Soup should be cooked through and flavors blended for another 2–3 minutes of cooking time.

Heat and enjoy as a refreshing soup.

Nutrients:

Calories: 80

Fat: 3g

Carbohydrates: 8g

Protein: 6g

11. Vegetarian Chow Mein

Items used:

- 8 oz chow mein noodles
- 1 tablespoon vegetable oil
- 1 cup shredded cabbage
- 1 cup julienned carrots
- 1 cup bean sprouts
- 1/2 cup sliced mushrooms
- 1/4 cup sliced scallions
- 2 cloves garlic, minced
- 1 tablespoon soy sauce
- 1 tablespoon oyster sauce (optional)
- Salt and pepper to taste

How to cook:

Noodles for chow mein should be prepared in accordance with package directions. Drain and put away.

Vegetable oil should be heated over high heat in a big pan or wok. To soften the vegetables, stir-fry them in the pan for two to three minutes after you've added the shredded cabbage, julienned carrots, bean sprouts, sliced mushrooms, sliced scallions, and chopped garlic.

Cooked chow mein noodles should be added to the veggie mixture in the pan.

To create the sauce, combine the soy sauce and oyster sauce (if using) in a small bowl and whisk until smooth.

Coat the chow mein and vegetables in the sauce, then pour it over the mixture in the pan.

Wait a minute or two more for the sauce to thicken and coat the noodles and vegetables.

Put in as much salt and pepper as you want.

This is a traditional Chinese noodle meal, so serve it hot.

Nutrients:

Calories: 300

Fat: 5g

Carbohydrates: 55g

Protein: 10g

12. Vegan Mongolian Tofu

Items used:

- 1 (14 oz) tofu
- 1/4 cup cornstarch
- 2 tablespoons vegetable oil
- 1/4 cup soy sauce
- 1/4 cup brown sugar
- 1/4 cup water
- 2 cloves garlic, minced
- 1/2 teaspoon grated ginger
- 1/4 teaspoon red pepper flakes
- 4 green onions, sliced

How to cook:

Cube the pressed, drained tofu into 1-inch pieces.

Cornstarch should be tossed with the tofu cubes until they are uniformly coated.

Vegetable oil should be heated over high heat in a big pan or wok. To get the tofu crispy and golden brown, add it to the pan after it has been coated and stir-fry for 5 to 7 minutes.

For the Mongolian sauce, combine the soy sauce, brown sugar, water, garlic, ginger, and red pepper flakes in a small bowl and whisk until smooth.

Toss the crispy tofu in the sauce and heat through.

Hold off on serving the tofu until the sauce has thickened and coated it entirely.

Slice some green onions and toss them into the skillet.

Leave the green onions in the pan for another minute or two to soften.

Sweet and flavorful, this dish is best served hot.

Nutrients:

Calories: 250

Fat: 10g

Carbohydrates: 25g

Protein: 15g

13. Vegan Sweet and Sour Vegetables

Items used:

- 1 tablespoon vegetable oil
- 1 large onion, chopped into large chunks
- 1 red bell pepper
- 1 green bell pepper
- 1 cup chopped pineapple
- 1 cup sliced carrots
- 1 cup sliced celery
- 2 cloves garlic, minced
- 1 tablespoon cornstarch
- 1/4 cup rice vinegar
- 1/4 cup brown sugar

- 1/4 cup ketchup
- 1/4 cup vegetable broth
- 1 tablespoon soy sauce
- Salt and pepper to taste

How to cook:

Vegetable oil should be heated over high heat in a big pan or wok. To soften them somewhat, stir-fry the chopped onion, red bell pepper, and green bell pepper for around 2 to 3 minutes.

Stir-fry the chicken for a few minutes, then add the pineapple, carrots, celery, and garlic and cook until the vegetables are tender.

Cornstarch, rice vinegar, brown sugar, ketchup, vegetable broth, and soy sauce are whisked together in a small dish to form the sweet and sour sauce.

Toss the veggies in the skillet with the sweet and sour sauce.

The vegetables should be left in the pan for another minute or two to be covered in the sauce and cooked through.

Put in as much salt and pepper as you want.

It's a vibrant and zesty meal that's best served hot.

Nutrients:

Calories: 200

Fat: 5g

Carbohydrates: 40g

Protein: 3g

14. Spicy Vegan Stir-fried Noodles

Items used:

- 8 oz noodles (linguine or rice noodles)
- 2 tablespoons vegetable oil
- 1 red bell pepper, sliced

- 1 yellow onion, sliced

- 2 cloves garlic, minced

- 1 red chili pepper, sliced

- 1/4 cup soy sauce

- 2 tablespoons rice vinegar

- 1 tablespoon brown sugar

- 1 teaspoon grated ginger

- Salt and pepper to taste

How to cook:

Noodles should be prepared according package directions. Drain and put away.

Vegetable oil should be heated over high heat in a big pan or wok. Stir-fry the red bell pepper, yellow onion, garlic, and red chili pepper for two to three minutes, or until the vegetables have cooked.

Cooked noodles should be added to the pan with the veggie mixture and stirred to incorporate.

To prepare the hot sauce, combine the soy sauce, rice vinegar, brown sugar, and ginger in a small bowl and whisk until smooth.

Mix the noodles and veggies with the hot sauce and toss them in a pan.

Wait a minute or two more for the sauce to thicken and coat the noodles and vegetables.

Put in as much salt and pepper as you want.

It's ready in a flash, so serve it hot.

Nutrients:

Calories: 300

Fat: 8g

Carbohydrates: 50g

Protein: 8g

15. Vegan Vegetable Dumplings

Items used:

- For the dumplings:
- 1 tablespoon vegetable oil
- 1/2 cup chopped onion
- 1/2 cup chopped cabbage
- 1/2 cup chopped carrots
- 1/2 cup chopped mushrooms
- 2 cloves garlic, minced
- 1 tablespoon soy sauce
- 1 tablespoon rice vinegar
- 1 teaspoon grated ginger
- 20 dumpling wrappers
- For the dipping sauce:
- 1/4 cup soy sauce
- 1 tablespoon rice vinegar
- 1 teaspoon sesame oil
- 1/2 teaspoon grated ginger
- 1/2 teaspoon red pepper flakes

How to cook:

Vegetable oil should be heated over medium-high heat in a large pan or wok. Stir-fry the onion, cabbage, carrots, mushrooms, and garlic for about 7 minutes, or until the vegetables have softened somewhat.

To create the sauce for the dumpling filling, combine the soy sauce, rice vinegar, and ginger in a deep bowl and whisk until smooth.

Combine the sauce from the dumpling filling with the veggies and toss.

The vegetables should be left in the pan for another minute or two to be covered in the sauce and cooked through.

Take the skillet from the heat and wait a few minutes for the filling to cool.

Fill each dumpling wrapper with a heaping teaspoonful of the filling.

Seal the contents inside by wetting the wrapper's edges and folding it in half.

Create a pleated look by pinching the wrapper's edges together.

Cook the dumplings for three to five minutes in a big saucepan of boiling water, or until they float to the top and the wrappers are well cooked.

In a large bowl, combine the ingredients for the dipping sauce: soy sauce, rice vinegar, sesame oil, grated ginger, with crushed red pepper flakes. Whisk the mixture until it is fully smooth.

Bring the dipping sauce and hot dumplings to the table.

Nutrients:

Calories: 150

Fat: 4g

Carbohydrates: 23g

Protein: 5g

CHAPTER 7

SAUCES AND CONDIMENTS

1. Soy Sauce

Items used:

- 1/4 cup soy sauce
- 1 tablespoon rice vinegar
- 1 teaspoon sesame oil
- 1/2 teaspoon grated ginger
- 1/2 teaspoon red pepper flakes (optional)

How to cook:

Combine the soy sauce, rice vinegar, sesame oil, ginger, and red pepper flakes (if using) in a small bowl and whisk to combine.

Use as a condiment for dipping sushi, dumplings, or other foods.

Nutrients:

Calories: 15

Fat: 1g

Carbohydrates: 1g

Protein: 1g

2. Hoisin Sauce

Items used:

- 1/4 cup soy sauce
- 2 tablespoons peanut butter
- 2 tablespoons honey
- 1 tablespoon rice vinegar
- 1 tablespoon sesame oil
- 1 clove garlic, minced
- 1/2 teaspoon grated ginger
- 1/4 teaspoon red pepper flakes (optional)

How to cook:

Combine the soy sauce, peanut butter, honey, rice vinegar, sesame oil, garlic, ginger, and red pepper flakes (if using) in a small bowl and stir to combine.

Use it to marinate meat, fish, or vegetables, or be creative and make a dipping sauce out of it.

Nutrients:

Calories: 120

Fat: 7g

Carbohydrates: 12g

Protein: 4g

3. Oyster Sauce

Items used:

- 1/4 cup soy sauce
- 1/4 cup vegetable broth

- 1 tablespoon sugar
- 1 tablespoon cornstarch
- 1 teaspoon sesame oil
- 1/2 teaspoon grated ginger
- 1/4 teaspoon garlic powder

How to cook:

Combine the soy sauce, vegetable broth, sugar, cornstarch, sesame oil, ginger, garlic, and garlic powder in a small saucepan and whisk until smooth.

Bring the contents of the saucepan up to a simmer over medium heat.

Continue cooking and stirring for another minute or two to thicken the sauce.

Remove the prepared sauce from the heat source. Then give it some time to settle for a while.

Vegan oyster sauce may be kept in the fridge for up to a week if stored in an airtight container.

Nutrients:

Calories: 35

Fat: 1g

Carbohydrates: 7g

Protein: 1g

4. Teriyaki Sauce

Items used:

- 1/2 cup soy sauce
- 1/2 cup brown sugar
- 1/4 cup water
- 2 tablespoons sake or dry white wine
- 1 tablespoon grated ginger
- 1 clove garlic, minced

How to cook:

Combine the soy sauce, brown sugar, water, sake or dry white wine, grated ginger, and chopped garlic in a small pot and stir to combine.

Bring the contents of the saucepan up to a simmer over medium heat.

Reduce the sauce by half and let it thicken in the pan for approximately 10 minutes, stirring regularly.

Remove the prepared sauce from the heat and let it rest.

In a jar that seals well, you may store the teriyaki sauce in the refrigerator for up to a week.

Nutrients:

Calories: 70

Fat: 0g

Carbohydrates: 17g

Protein: 1g

5. Szechuan Sauce

Items used:

- 1/4 cup soy sauce
- 2 tablespoons rice vinegar
- 1 tablespoon sesame oil
- 1 tablespoon honey
- 1 tablespoon chili garlic sauce
- 1 teaspoon grated ginger
- 1/2 teaspoon Szechuan peppercorns, crushed
- 1/4 teaspoon garlic powder

How to cook:

Soy sauce, rice vinegar, sesame oil, honey, chili garlic sauce, grated ginger, crushed Szechuan peppercorns, and garlic powder are mixed together in a small bowl.

Use as a delicious marinade or dipping sauce for meat, seafood, or vegetables.

Nutrients:

Calories: 60

Fat: 4g

Carbohydrates: 5g

Protein: 1g

6. Peanut Sauce

Items used:

- 1/2 cup creamy peanut butter
- 2 tablespoons soy sauce
- 2 tablespoons rice vinegar
- 1 tablespoon maple syrup
- 1 clove garlic, minced
- 1/4 teaspoon red pepper flakes (optional)
- 1/4 cup water

How to cook:

Peanut butter, soy sauce, rice vinegar, maple syrup, chopped garlic, and optional red pepper flakes may be combined in a small bowl and whisked together.

Slowly add water while whisking until the sauce reaches the desired thickness.

Use as a delicious condiment on sandwiches or as a salad dressing.

Nutrients:

Calories: 140

Fat: 10g

Carbohydrates: 8g

Protein: 6g

7. Sweet and Sour Sauce

Items used:

- 3/4 cup sugar
- 2/3 cup water
- 1/3 cup white vinegar
- 1/4 cup ketchup
- 1 tablespoon soy sauce
- 2 tablespoons cornstarch

How to cook:

Stir the sugar, water, white vinegar, ketchup, and soy sauce together in a small pot.

Bring the contents of the saucepan up to a simmer over medium heat.

In a small dish, dissolve the cornstarch by whisking together 2 tablespoons of water and the cornstarch till the cornstarch is completely dissolved.

To get the desired consistency for the sauce, gradually incorporate the cornstarch mixture into the saucepan while whisking it.

Take the sauce off the stove and allow it to cool to room temperature before serving.

The sweet and sour sauce may be kept in a fridge for a week if it is placed in a container that does not allow air to circulate around it.

Nutrients:

Calories: 70

Fat: 0g

Carbohydrates: 18g

Protein: 0g

8. Chili Oil

Items used:

- 1 cup vegetable oil
- 1/2 cup chili flakes
- 1 tablespoon Szechuan peppercorns
- 1 teaspoon salt
- 1 tablespoon sugar
- 2 cloves garlic, minced
- 1/2 teaspoon grated ginger

How to cook:

Vegetable oil should be heated in a deep saucepan over medium flame until it is hot to the touch but not smoking.

Mix the chili flakes, Szechuan peppercorns, salt, sugar, garlic, and ginger in a heat-safe bowl.

The chili mixture is ready; now pour the heated oil over it and whisk to blend.

The oil should be room temperature before using.

Store the Chile oil in the fridge for up to a month.

Nutrients:

Calories: 120

Fat: 14g

Carbohydrates: 1g

Protein: 0g

9. Plum Sauce

Items used:

- 1 cup dried plums, pitted
- 1/2 cup water
- 2 tablespoons rice vinegar

- 2 tablespoons brown sugar
- 1/4 cup orange juice
- 1 teaspoon finely minced shallot

How to cook:

Dry the plums and add them to a small saucepan with the water, rice vinegar, brown sugar, orange juice, and chopped shallot.

Over medium heat, bring the liquid to a boil.

Sauté over low heat for approximately 10 to 15 minutes, or until the plums have reached the desired tenderness and the sauce has reached the desired consistency.

Take the plum sauce from the stove and let it cool.

The plum sauce may be stored in the fridge for up to a week if stored in an airtight container.

Nutrients:

Calories: 70

Fat: 0g

Carbohydrates: 18g

Protein: 1g

10. Satay Sauce

Items used:

- 1/2 cup creamy peanut butter
- 1/2 cup coconut milk
- 2 tablespoons soy sauce
- 2 tablespoons lime juice
- 1 tablespoon brown sugar
- 1 clove garlic, minced
- 1/4 teaspoon ground ginger

How to cook:

Add the peanut butter, coconut milk, soy sauce, lime juice, brown sugar, minced garlic, and ground ginger to a small saucepan and stir to combine.

Bring the contents of the saucepan up to a simmer over medium heat.

To thicken the sauce, let it simmer for 5-10 minutes while stirring periodically.

Take the satay sauce from the stove and set it aside to cool.

Put the satay sauce in a jar and enjoy!

Nutrients:

Calories: 140

Fat: 11g

Carbohydrates: 7g

Protein: 5g

11. Black Bean Sauce

Items used:

- 1 cup fermented black beans
- 1/3 cup vegetable oil
- 1/4 cup finely chopped garlic
- 2 tablespoons chopped ginger
- 2-3 shallots, chopped
- 2-3 dried chili peppers, chopped
- 1 tablespoon soy sauce
- 1 tablespoon sugar

How to cook:

Drain and re-rinse the fermented black beans under cold water.

Vegetable oil should be heated over medium heat in a small saucepan.

In a saucepan, combine the minced garlic, ginger, shallots, and dried chili flakes.

To get a pleasant aroma and tender veggies, cook stirring periodically.

To the pot, whisk in the fermented black beans and continue cooking for another two to three minutes.

Add the soy sauce and sugar and simmer, stirring periodically, for another minute or two.

Take the black bean sauce off the stove and let it cool.

Put the black bean sauce in a jar and enjoy!

Nutrients:

Calories: 120

Fat: 10g

Carbohydrates: 7g

Protein: 3g

12. Sesame Sauce

Items used:

- 1/2 cup sesame seeds
- 1/4 cup soy sauce
- 2 tablespoons rice vinegar
- 1 tablespoon maple syrup
- 1 clove garlic, minced
- 1/4 teaspoon ground ginger
- 1/4 cup water

How to cook:

The sesame seeds need to be toasted in a small pan over medium heat until they are golden and aromatic.

Blend or process the toasted sesame seeds, soy sauce, rice vinegar, maple syrup, garlic, ginger, and water in a small blender or food processor until smooth.

Make sure to blend it until it's nice and creamy.

The sesame sauce may be stored in the fridge for up to a week if stored in an airtight container.

Nutrients:

Calories: 120

Fat: 9g

Carbohydrates: 7g

Protein: 4g

13. Ponzu Sauce

Items used:

- 1 tablespoon mirin
- 2 tablespoons sake
- 3 tablespoons freshly squeezed citrus juice (lemon, lime, or orange)
- 1/3 cup soy sauce
- 2 tablespoons rice vinegar

How to cook:

Combine the mirin, sake, freshly squeezed citrus juice, soy sauce, and rice vinegar in a deep bowl and whisk to combine.

The ponzu sauce may be stored in the fridge for up to a week if kept in an airtight container.

Nutrients:

Calories: 30

Fat: 0g

Carbohydrates: 3g

Protein: 2g

14. Mushroom Sauce

Items used:

- 2 tablespoons olive oil
- 1 large onion, diced
- 4 cloves garlic, minced
- 1 pound mushrooms, sliced
- 1/2 cup vegetable broth
- 2 tablespoons soy sauce
- 1 tablespoon nutritional yeast
- 1/2 teaspoon dried thyme
- Salt and pepper, to taste

How to cook:

To get started, place the olive oil in a big pan and bring it up to temperature over medium heat.

After the oil has heated up, add the onion and garlic and continue to sauté for two to three minutes while stirring often. This should continue until the onion and garlic give off their scent and become slightly softer.

Sliced mushrooms should be added to the pan at this point and cooked for another 5 to 7 minutes, stirring periodically, until they are soft and browned.

Add the soy sauce, nutritional yeast, dried thyme, salt, and pepper to the vegetable broth and mix well until the sauce thickens.

Take the mushroom sauce off the stove and let it cool for a while.

Store the mushroom sauce in the fridge for a week in a clean and an airtight container.

Nutrients:

Calories: 80

Fat: 5g

Carbohydrates: 7g

Protein: 3g

15. Curry Paste

Items used:

- 2 tablespoons coriander seeds
- 2 tablespoons cumin seeds
- 1 tablespoon fennel seeds
- 1 teaspoon black peppercorns
- 2 dried red chilies
- 1 shallot, chopped
- 4 cloves garlic, chopped
- 1 tablespoon grated ginger
- 2 tablespoons tomato paste
- 2 tablespoons vegetable oil
- 1 teaspoon salt

How to cook:

Over medium heat, with the occasional stir, toast the coriander seeds, cumin seeds, fennel seeds, and black peppercorns in a small pan until aromatic.

Toss the toasted spices, dried red chilies, shallot, garlic, ginger, tomato paste, vegetable oil, and salt into a mini food processor or blender.

Make sure to blend it until it's nice and creamy.

Put the curry paste in a jar and enjoy!

Nutrients:

Calories: 40

Fat: 3g

Carbohydrates: 3g

Protein: 1g

CHAPTER 8

DESSERTS

1. Mango Sticky Rice

Items used:

- 1 cup glutinous (sweet) rice
- 1 1/4 cups canned unsweetened coconut milk
- 1/2 cup sugar
- 1/4 teaspoon salt
- 2 ripe mangoes, peeled and sliced
- Toasted sesame seeds, for garnish

How to cook:

Drain and re-rinse the sticky rice with cold water.

Over high heat, bring 1 1/2 cups of water and the glutinous rice to a boil in a medium saucepan.

Simmer over low flame, with the lid on, for fifteen to twenty minutes, or till the rice has become tender and all of the water has been soaked (whichever comes first).

Bring the unsweetened coconut milk from a can, the sugar, and the salt to a boil in a small saucepan over medium heat.

Simmer on low for about seven minutes, or until the sauce has thickened.

Cooked glutinous rice should be mixed with half of the coconut milk sauce in a big dish.

Let the rice cool to room temperature in the covered bowl.

Sticky rice with sliced mangoes may be served as an appetizer or a main dish.

Sprinkle the mangoes with the toasted sesame seeds and any leftover coconut milk sauce.

Nutrients:

Calories: 350

Fat: 12g

Carbohydrates: 60g

Protein: 3g

2. Chinese Egg Tarts

Items used:

- For the pastry:
- 1 stick (4 ounces) unsalted butter, softened
- 1/2 cup granulated sugar
- 1/2 teaspoon salt
- 1 large egg
- 1 1/2 cups all-purpose flour
- For the custard filling:
- 2 large eggs
- 1/2 cup granulated sugar
- 1 cup whole milk
- 1/2 teaspoon vanilla extract

How to cook:

Softened unsalted butter, granulated sugar, and salt should be creamed together in a large basin until pale and fluffy.

Blend in the jumbo egg with a mixer.

Add the all-purpose flour little by little and mix until a dough forms.

To make 12 muffins, cut the dough in half and put each half into a greased muffin cup.

Large eggs, sugar, whole milk, and vanilla essence are whisked together in a medium bowl.

Fill the pastry shells with the custard filling to roughly 3/4 of their capacity.

Egg tarts need 20-25 minutes in a preheated 375°F oven to get a golden brown color and a firm custard.

When the egg tarts may be withdrawn from their ovens and given time to cool to ambient temperature, they are ready to be served.

The egg tarts should be served straight from the muffin pan, but you may also place them on a serving tray.

Nutrients:

Calories: 240

Fat: 12g

Carbohydrates: 29g

Protein: 4g

3. Sesame Balls

Items used:

- 1 cup glutinous rice flour
- 1/4 cup sugar
- 1/2 cup water
- 1/2 cup sweet red bean paste
- 1/2 cup sesame seeds

- Vegetable oil, for frying

How to cook:

To make a smooth dough, mix the glutinous rice flour, sugar, and water in a big bowl.

Roll the dough into 12 balls and divide them evenly.

Flatten each ball using your fingers and fill it with some of the wonderful red bean paste.

Seal the filling inside by pinching the dough together, then roll the ball between your hands to smooth out any imperfections.

Press the sesame seeds firmly into the dough as you roll each ball in them.

Vegetable oil should be heated over medium heat in a big skillet.

Deep fry the sesame balls in oil.

Using a slotted spoon, transfer the sesame balls off the pan to a plate covered with paper towels to absorb any remaining oil.

You may eat the sesame balls warm or cold.

Nutrients:

Calories: 180

Fat: 7g

Carbohydrates: 27g

Protein: 3g

4. Matcha Ice Cream

Items used:

- 2 cups whole milk
- 1 cup heavy cream
- 5 large egg yolks
- 3/4 cup granulated sugar
- 1/4 teaspoon salt
- 5 tablespoons matcha tea powder

How to cook:

Combine the whole milk and the heavy cream in a pan and cook over a medium-high flame until hot but not boiling, stirring occasionally.

In a deep bowl, combine the egg yolks with the sugar, salt, and matcha tea powder

Slowly pour the prepared hot milk mixture into the bowl containing the egg yolks, stirring constantly so as not to scramble the eggs.

Stirring often, simmer the mixture over low heat for 10 to 12 minutes or until it thickens enough to stick to the tip of a spoon.

Take the mixture from the heat and pour it into a big bowl through a fine-mesh strainer.

Put the bowl in the fridge for at least two hours, or maybe overnight, to cool.

After the mixture has cold, pour it into an ice cream machine and churn it as directed.

The ice cream may be frozen for at least 2 hours, or perhaps overnight, once it has been churned.

Nutrients:

Calories: 300

Fat: 19g

Carbohydrates: 28g

Protein: 6g

5. Pineapple Upside-Down Cake

Items used:

- 1/4 cup unsalted butter, melted
- 1/2 cup packed light brown sugar
- 2 cups fresh cubed pineapple, cut into pieces
- 1 1/2 cups all-purpose flour
- 1 teaspoon baking powder
- 1/2 teaspoon baking soda
- 1/4 teaspoon salt

- 1/2 cup unsalted butter, softened
- 1 cup granulated sugar
- 2 large eggs
- 1 teaspoon vanilla extract
- 1/2 cup milk

How to cook:

Prepare a 350F oven.

Spread the melted unsalted butter and the packed light brown sugar in a 9-inch cake pan.

Spread a single layer of fresh pineapple cubes over the brown sugar.

Mix the all-purpose flour, baking powder, baking soda, and salt together in a medium basin.

Softened unsalted butter and granulated sugar should be creamed together in a large bowl until pale and fluffy.

The big eggs should be added one at a time and beaten in between additions.

Add the vanilla essence and mix well.

Adding the flour mixture and the milk in turns, whisk until a smooth batter is formed.

The batter should be poured and distributed evenly over the pineapple in the cake pan.

To test doneness, stick a toothpick into the middle of the cake and remove it cleanly. Bake in the oven for 45 to 50 minutes.

Take the delicious cake out of the oven and let it cool.

Once the cake has cooled fully, invert it onto a serving dish.

Nutrients:

Calories: 350

Fat: 16g

Carbohydrates: 49g

Protein: 4g

6. Fried Bananas

Items used:

- 4 ripe bananas, sliced 1 inch thick
- 2 tablespoons all-purpose flour
- 3/4 cup all-purpose flour
- 1/2 cup granulated sugar
- 1/2 teaspoon baking powder
- 1/4 teaspoon salt
- 1/2 cup water
- Vegetable oil, for frying

How to cook:

Two tablespoons of all-purpose flour, three-quarters of a cup of all-purpose flour, granulated sugar, baking powder, and salt should be mixed together in a big basin.

To get a smooth batter, add the water gradually while stirring.

Coat each piece of sliced banana in the batter.

Vegetable oil should be heated over medium heat in a big skillet.

The bananas need around 3 minutes of frying time each side in the batter to get an attractive golden brown and crisp appearance.

With a slotted spoon, transfer the fried bananas to a plate lined with paper towels, where they can soak up any excess oil.

Offer the fried bananas warm, dusted with powdered sugar or drizzled with honey, if desired.

Nutrients:

Calories: 250

Fat: 8g

Carbohydrates: 44g

Protein: 2g

7. Coconut Rice Pudding

Items used:

- 1 cup short-grain white rice
- 1 can (14 ounces) coconut milk
- 2 cups whole milk
- 1/2 cup granulated sugar
- 1/4 teaspoon salt
- 1 teaspoon vanilla extract
- Fresh fruit or nuts, for topping

How to cook:

Bring the white rice, coconut milk, whole milk, sugar, and salt to a boil over medium heat in a large saucepan.

The rice should be soft and the sauce rich and creamy after 30–40 minutes of simmering over low heat with occasional stirring.

Turn off the stove and add the vanilla essence to the pan.

When the rice pudding has reached room temperature, place it in a serving dish.

If you choose, you may put some fresh fruit or nuts on top of the rice pudding.

The coconut rice pudding is great both cold and at room temperature.

Nutrients:

Calories: 300

Fat: 14g

Carbohydrates: 40g

Protein: 5g

8. Almond Cookies

Items used:

- 1 1/3 cups whole almonds (or 2 cups of ground almonds)
- 1/2 cup + 1 tablespoon granulated sugar
- 1/4 cup all-purpose flour
- 1/4 teaspoon salt
- 1/4 cup unsalted butter, softened
- 1 large egg white
- 1/2 teaspoon almond extract

How to cook:

Prepare a 350F oven.

Whole almonds may be processed into a fine powder in a food processor.

Ground almonds, sugar, flour, and salt should be mixed together in a big basin using a whisk.

Mix in the egg white and almond essence with the unsalted butter that has been melted.

Form the dough into 1-inch balls, then lay them, parchment-side up, on a baking sheet.

Flatten each ball gently using your hand.

Bake the cookies for 12-15 minutes after preheating the oven.

After a duration of 5 minutes, extract the baked goods from the oven and permit them to cool on the sheet of parchment paper.

The cookies should be cooled on a wire rack.

Nutrients:

Calories: 120

Fat: 8g

Carbohydrates: 10g

Protein: 3g

98

9. Fried Sesame Balls

Items used:

- 1 cup glutinous rice flour
- 1/2 cup water
- 1/4 cup granulated sugar
- 1/2 cup delicious red bean paste or sesame paste
- 1/4 cup white sesame seeds
- Vegetable oil, for frying

How to cook:

To make a smooth dough, combine glutinous rice flour, water, and sugar in a big bowl.

Divide the dough into 12 equal halves and roll each into a ball.

Flatten each ball with your fingers, and then fill it with savoury red bean spread or sesame paste.

Seal the filling inside by pinching the dough together, then roll the ball between your hands to smooth it out.

Press the white sesame seeds into the dough as you roll each ball in them.

Vegetable oil

Deep minutes each side, or until golden brown and crispy, fry the sesame balls in oil.

Fry the sesame balls until golden brown

, then remove them from the pan with a spoon that is slotted and drain them on paper towels.

It's best to serve the crispy sesame balls steaming hot.

Nutrients:

Calories: 150

Fat: 6g

Carbohydrates: 23g

Protein: 2g

10. Japanese Cheesecake

Items used:

- 4 large eggs, separated
- 4 tablespoons butter
- 1 (8-ounce) block full-fat cream cheese
- 1/4 cup heavy cream
- 1/4 cup granulated sugar
- 1/4 cup all-purpose flour
- 1 tablespoon cornstarch
- 1 teaspoon vanilla extract

How to cook:

Put in a preheated 325 degree oven.

Line the cake pan (about 8 inches in diameter) with parchment paper and grease the pan with unsalted butter.

Egg whites should be beaten with an electric mixer in a large bowl until firm peaks form.

Unsalted butter, full-fat cream cheese, and heavy cream should be beaten together in a separate large basin using an electric mixer until smooth.

Mix in the vanilla extract, cornstarch, all-purpose flour, and granulated sugar until everything is evenly distributed.

The egg yolks should be added to the bowl and mixed together thoroughly.

Carefully incorporate the whisk egg whites into the cream cheese mixture.

Then, using a spatula, spread the batter evenly over the surface of the cake pan.

Wrap carefully the outside of the pan in aluminum foil, then place it into a bigger baking dish that can hold boiling water up to halfway up the sides of the cake pan.

Pre-heat the oven to 350 degrees and bake the cheesecake or until the top is golden and the cheesecake is set.

Put the cheesecake on a cooling rack and turn off the oven.

It's best to let the cheesecake chill in the fridge before cutting into it.

Nutrients:

Calories: 300

Fat: 23g

Carbohydrates: 17g

Protein: 7g

11. Bubble Tea

Items used:

- 1/4 cup dried boba tapioca pearls
- 1 to 2 tea bags, any kind
- 1/2 cup water
- 1/2 cup milk or non-dairy milk
- 1 tablespoon honey or sugar, or to taste
- Ice cubes

How to cook:

Two cups of water should be boil well in a small pot set over high heat.

Stir the dried boba tapioca pearls into the boiled water.

Cook the boba for 5-10 minutes on medium heat, or until soft and chewy.

The boba should be drained and then rinsed in cold water.

Separately, bring half a cup of water to a boil over high heat in a separate pot.

Steep the tea bags in water that has been brought to a boil for three to five minutes, or until the tea has reached the desired strength and taste.

Take out the tea bags and melt the sugar or honey by stirring.

Put some ice cubes and the finished boba in a glass.

The boba and ice should be doused in the sweetened tea.

To a glass, pour the milk (or non-dairy milk) and give it a little toss.

The chewy boba in bubble tea is best experienced with a broad straw.

Nutrients:

Calories: 150

Fat: 3g

Carbohydrates: 30g

Protein: 2g

12. Thai Coconut Pancakes

Items used:

- 1 cup rice flour
- 2 teaspoons tapioca flour
- 1/2 cup cooked jasmine rice
- 1 15-ounce can coconut milk
- 1/2 cup granulated sugar
- 1/4 teaspoon salt
- 1/4 cup coconut cream

How to cook:

Rice flour, tapioca flour, cooked jasmine rice, coconut milk, granulated sugar, and salt should all be mixed together in a big basin using a whisk.

Over medium heat, preheat a kanom krok or aebleskiver pan.

Spray or oil the pan to prepare it for cooking.

Fill the muffin cups approximately three-quarters of the way with the batter.

The pancakes are done when the edges are crispy and the centers are set, usually after 2 to 3 minutes in the oven.

The pancakes may be carefully lifted off the pan and placed on a dish using a tiny spoon or fork.

To use up the rest of the batter, start again.

Warm the coconut cream in a small saucepan over low heat.

Serve the pancakes immediately with the warm coconut cream drizzled on top.

Nutrients:

Calories: 200

Fat: 7g

Carbohydrates: 33g

Protein: 2g

13. Fruit Spring Rolls

Items used:

- 8 rice paper wrappers
- 1 kiwi, sliced
- 1/4 cup strawberries, sliced
- 1/2 mango, sliced
- 1/4 cup raspberries
- 1/2 green apple, sliced
- 1/4 cup honey
- 1/4 cup plain Greek yogurt
- 1 tablespoon lime juice

How to cook:

Get a big basin and fill it with hot water.

Soften rice paper by dipping it in water for 5-10 seconds.

Spread the pliable rice paper wrapping out on a tidy table.

Place some fruit slices in the middle of the rice paper wrapper. Try some green apple, kiwi, strawberry, mango, and raspberry slices.

Roll the fruit securely in the rice paper, folding in the sides.

Use the remaining fruit and rice paper wrappers in a similar fashion.

Honey, plain Greek yogurt, and lime juice should be mixed together in a basin.

To accompany the fruit spring rolls, pass the dipping sauce.

Nutrients:

Calories: 120

Fat: 0g

Carbohydrates: 30g

Protein: 2g

14. Chinese Steamed Sponge Cake

Items used:

- 5 large eggs, at room temperature
- 3/4 cup granulated sugar
- 1 cup cake flour
- 1/2 teaspoon baking powder (optional)
- Pinch of salt
- 1 teaspoon vanilla extract

How to cook:

Eggs and sugar should be beaten together in a large bowl until light and fluffy.

The cake flour, baking powder, and a pinch of salt should be shifted into the basin before being gently folded in.

Add the vanilla essence and mix well.

Use a greased 8-inch cake pan to place the batter.

To eliminate air bubbles, tap the cake pan on the counter lightly.

Steam the cake pan in a steamer basket over high heat until a toothpick inserted in the cake comes out clean.

Take the cake pan out of the steamer and set it down on a cooling rack to cool completely.

Loosen the prepared cake from the sides of the pan with a knife, then flip it over onto a serving platter.

Cut the Chinese steamed sponge cake into slices and serve.

Nutrients:

Calories: 180

Fat: 3g

Carbohydrates: 33g

Protein: 5g

15. Korean Sweet Pancakes (Hotteok)

Items used:

- 1 1/4 cups all-purpose flour
- 1/2 cup sweet rice flour
- 1 tsp instant yeast
- 1/4 cup granulated sugar
- 1/2 tsp salt
- 1/2 cup warm milk
- 1/4 cup vegetable oil
- 1/2 cup brown sugar
- 1 tsp ground cinnamon
- 1/2 cup chopped nuts (optional)

How to cook:

Mix the all-purpose flour, sweet rice flour, instant yeast, sugar, and salt in a large basin.

Stir in the heated milk and vegetable oil until a dough forms, about a minute.

On a fully floured surface, knead the dough for 5-10 minutes, or until it is smooth and elastic.

Let the dough rest under a wet towel for 30 minutes.

Brown sugar, ground cinnamon, and optional chopped nuts should be combined in a small bowl.

Cut the dough into eight or ten pieces.

Make a disc with each dough scrap and fill it with a heaping teaspoon of the brown sugar mixture.

Seal the filling within by pinching the dough together.

Prepare a medium fire in a skillet that won't stick.

Place the dough balls in the pan and cook until the dough is golden brown and the filling is cooked through.

Hot Korean sweet pancakes should be served.

Nutrients:

Calories: 250

Fat: 11g

Carbohydrates: 34g

Protein: 4g

CHAPTER 9

DRINKS

1. Green Tea

Items used:

- 1 green tea bag
- 1 cup hot water

How to cook:

Heat one cup of water to a rolling boil.

Take it off the heat when the internal temperature hits 190 degrees Fahrenheit and let it sit for a while.

Get yourself a cup and a green tea bag.

Submerge the tea bag in the boiling water.

Prepare a 3-4 minute infusion.

It's time to drink your Green Tea, so take out the tea bag.

Nutrients:

Calories: 0

Fat: 0g

Carbohydrates: 0g

Protein: 0g

2. Hong Kong Milk Tea

Items used:

- 2 black tea bags
- 2 cups water
- 1/2 cup evaporated milk
- 2 tbsp sugar (optional)

How to cook:

Heat up two cups of water until it boils.

Prepare a cup of black tea by steeping two tea bags in hot water for five to ten minutes.

Bring out the tea bags from the cup and pour in half a cup of evaporated milk.

Add 2 tablespoons of sugar (optional) and mix until sugar is dissolved.

Hong Kong milk tea may be served either hot or cold, over ice.

Nutrients:

Calories: 120

Fat: 4g

Carbohydrates: 17g

Protein: 5g

3. Vietnamese Iced Coffee

Items used:

- 2 tbsp dark roast coffee grounds
- 2 tbsp sweetened condensed milk
- 1 cup ice
- 1 cup hot water

How to cook:

Prepare a pot of Vietnamese coffee by combining 2 tablespoons of coffee grounds with 1 cup of boiling water in a French press.

Dissolve 2 tablespoons of sweetened condensed milk by stirring it into the coffee.

Put 1 cup of ice cubes into a glass.

The ice should be topped with the coffee mixture.

Give the Vietnamese Iced Coffee a good stir and savor it.

Nutrients:

Calories: 120

Fat: 3g

Carbohydrates: 21g

Protein: 3g

4. Thai Iced Tea

Items used:

- 2 tbsp loose-leaf black tea
- 1 pod star anise
- 2 pods cardamom
- 1/2 cinnamon stick (optional)
- 1/8 vanilla bean (optional)
- 1/4 cup sweetened condensed milk

- 1/4 cup evaporated milk
- 1 cup ice

How to cook:

Black tea, star anise, cardamom pods, a cinnamon stick, and a vanilla bean (if used) should be combined with 4 cups of water in a medium pot.

Bring the ingredients to a boil, then lower the heat and boil well.

Take the pan from the stove and let it to cool for about 15 minutes.

Pour the tea into a clean pitcher.

Combine a quarter cup of evaporated milk with a quarter cup of sweetened condensed milk in a pitcher.

Put 1 cup of ice cubes into a glass.

Combine the ice and Thai iced tea.

Thai iced tea is best enjoyed after being stirred to combine the sugar and milk.

Nutrients:

Calories: 120

Fat: 3g

Carbohydrates: 21g

Protein: 3g

5. Mango Lassi

Items used:

- 1 cup chopped ripe mango
- 1 cup plain yogurt
- 1/2 cup milk
- 2 tbsp sugar
- 1/4 tsp ground cardamom
- 1 cup ice

How to cook:

Blend together 1/2 cup of milk, 2 tablespoons of sugar, 1/4 teaspoon of powder cardamom, and 1 cup of diced ripe mango.

Mix it up and get it as smooth as possible.

Blend in another cup of ice until the mixture is completely smooth.

To serve, fill a glass with the Mango Lassi.

Mango Lassi is served for its sweet and creamy flavor.

Nutrients:

Calories: 150

Fat: 3g

Carbohydrates: 26g

Protein: 7g

6. Lychee Martini

Items used:

- Ice
- 6 oz vodka
- 4 oz lychee juice or syrup reserved from the can of lychee
- 1 oz vermouth
- 2 lychee for garnish

How to cook:

Put ice cubes in a cocktail shaker.

To a cocktail shaker, pour 6 ounces of vodka, 4 ounces of the lychee juice or syrup set aside from the can, and 1 ounce of vermouth.

Get the drink cold by shaking it.

A cool martini glass is ideal for sipping the strained Lychee Martini.

Add two lychees as a garnish.

Lychee Martini is served and enjoyed for its delicious and refreshing flavor.

Nutrients:

Calories: 200

Fat: 0g

Carbohydrates: 12g

Protein: 0g

7. Sake Cocktail

Items used:

- 2 oz sake
- 2 oz fruit juice (such as pineapple or orange)
- 1 oz simple syrup
- Ice
- Fruit for garnish (optional)

How to cook:

Put ice cubes in a cocktail shaker.

Mix 1 ounce of simple syrup with 2 ounces each of sake and fruit juice in a cocktail shaker.

Get the drink cold by shaking it.

The Sake cocktail should be strained into a cold glass.

Add fruit as a garnish (if desired).

Sake Cocktail has a fruity, refreshing flavor that's perfect for serving and drinking.

Nutrients:

Calories: 150

Fat: 0g

Carbohydrates: 20g

Protein: 0g

8. Ginger Beer

Items used:

- 1 cup granulated sugar
- 1/2 cup water
- 2 tbsp grated fresh ginger
- 1/8 tsp active dry yeast
- 3 cups sparkling water
- Ice
- Lime wedges for garnish (optional)

How to cook:

One cup of granulated sugar, half a cup of water, and two tablespoons of grated fresh ginger should be combined in a small pot.

Boil the mixture and whisk periodically to dissolve the sugar.

Put the pot aside and allow it to cool to room temperature.

Stir in 1/8 teaspoon of active dry yeast until well incorporated.

Combine all of the ingredients and place them in a big glass jar, covering it with cheesecloth or a clean dish towel.

The combination has to set out for 24 to 48 hours at room temperature to become mildly alcoholic and effervescent.

Pour the strained Ginger Beer into a huge container.

To the Ginger Beer, gradually pour three cups of carbonated water and mix well.

Glasses should be filled with ice, and the Ginger Beer mixture should be poured over the top.

Add lime wedges as a garnish (if desired).

Ginger Beer is served and enjoyed for its fiery and refreshing flavor.

Nutrients:

Calories: 120

Fat: 0g

Carbohydrates: 31g

Protein: 0g

9. Bubble Tea

Items used:

- 1/4 cup dried boba tapioca pearls per serving
- 1 to 2 tea bags per serving, any kind
- 1/2 cup water
- 1/2 cup milk
- 2 tbsp sweetened condensed milk
- 2 tbsp simple syrup
- Ice

How to cook:

Boba tapioca pearls should be prepared as directed on the packet.

Cooked boba tapioca pearls and 2 tablespoons of simple syrup go into a glass.

Prepare a half cup of iced tea by steeping one or two tea bags in the water.

Combine half a cup of milk and two tablespoons of sweetened condensed milk in a separate glass.

The boba tapioca pearls and simple syrup should be mixed with ice, and then served.

To serve, pour the iced tea over the boba tapioca pearls and ice.

Add the milk and sugar to the tea.

Bubble Tea, please be stirred and enjoyed.

Nutrients:

Calories: 250

Fat: 4g

Carbohydrates: 50g

Protein: 4g

10. Lemonade

Items used:

- 1 cup granulated sugar
- 1 cup water
- 1 cup freshly squeezed lemon juice (from about 6 lemons)
- 4 cups water
- Ice
- Lemon slices for garnish (optional)

How to cook:

Put one cup of granulated sugar and one cup of water in a small pot and start heating it up.

To dissolve the sugar, boil the liquid in a saucepan over medium heat, stirring periodically.

Take the pot from the stove and set it aside until it reaches room temperature.

After the sugar syrup has cooled, add 1 cup of freshly squeezed lemon juice to a big pitcher.

Pour four cups of water into the pitcher and mix well.

For best results, refrigerate the lemonade for at least an hour before serving.

Put ice in the cups and pour the lemonade on top.

Slice a lemon for decoration (not required).

Serve up some refreshing lemonade and soak up the sun.

Nutrients:

Calories: 120

Fat: 0g

Carbohydrates: 31g

Protein: 0g

CONCLUSION

Wok cooking is a fun and exciting way to try new foods from all around the globe. The wok is an essential kitchen appliance for every home chef, whether their goal is to whip up a fast weekday dinner or to prepare a multi-course feast for visitors. We've included a wide variety of recipes for rice and noodles, meats and poultry, seafood, vegetarian and vegan alternatives, condiments, sweets, and beverages in this cookbook. Essential stir-frying, deep-frying, steaming, and smoking methods, as well as the background and culture of wok cooking, have been discussed. Inspiring you to try new tastes and methods in your own kitchen, this cookbook showcases the versatility and culinary potential of the wok. Enjoy your meal!

Printed in Great Britain
by Amazon

24178385R00071